SORT YOUR S-H-I-T OUT!
by
RYAN NURSE

Copyright © November 2023 Ryan Nurse
All rights reserved. This book or any portion thereof may not be reproduced or used in any manner whatsoever without the express written permission of the publisher except for the use of brief quotations in a book review.

Published by Mabel & Stanley Publishing

Scan this QR code with a camera or QR App to join our FB community and stay accountable on your journey.

Disclaimer

The tips and advice shared in this book are drawn from the personal experiences of Ryan Nurse and are meant to inspire and motivate readers in their pursuit of a fulfilling life. However, it is crucial to recognise that the suggestions provided are not a substitute for professional medical advice. If you are facing mental health difficulties or any medical concerns, it is strongly advised to consult with a qualified healthcare professional, the content of this book should not replace personalised medical guidance.

Readers are reminded that the advice offered does not guarantee specific results, and individual outcomes may vary - personal development is a unique journey, and results are subject to individual circumstances.

This book draws on quotes from Ryan's personal mindset coaching journey (many of which are paraphrased) for which original origins are unknown due to accumulated insights over time. The aim is to share collective wisdom with immense gratitude to unknown contributors.

Acknowledgements

I am deeply grateful to all the individuals who have contributed to the creation of this book, and to you for investing your priceless time to consume and comprehend all the contents within.

First and foremost, I want to express my heartfelt thanks to my parents for always being there for me, especially throughout my darkest of days which you'll find out more about in the following pages. The facts are that if it wasn't for them then you would not be reading these words right now.

Secondly, I would like to give special appreciation to those who once caused me tremendous pain in the past, because if it wasn't for them then I would never have learned the priceless life lessons I share with you in this book, and would never have been able to evolve into the person who I am today.

I am indebted to all my family and close friends for their consistent unwavering support throughout my journey so far, and am super excited to connect with all my future friends and acquaintances along this epic expedition I've embarked on.

Testimonials

"I first met Ryan online after he reached out to me on TikTok. I was impressed by his tenacity and I was even more impressed with the way he was committed to taking action.

We later connected further through the app Clubhouse and eventually we met in person. I was so pleased to discover that Ryan was exactly the same kind-hearted and genuine guy in person as he was online.

I respect the way that he is always willing to listen and learn from others and how he consistently 'shows up'. He is committed to helping others and always delivers great value based on his personal experience. I love how he is living his life on purpose and the fact that he is super courageous when it comes to taking massive action.

I am so pleased that he has written this book in order to share his all-important message with even more people and I am absolutely certain that it will bring clarity and inspiration to other individuals looking to level up and live their best lives!"

Simon Squibb:
Entrepreneur
Angel Investor
Founder of HelpBnk

"When I first met Ryan I was magnetised by his consistent energy and his indomitable spirit. Having learned he survived a near death experience and what he went through to live after being told he wouldn't is truly incredible!

What is more incredible is how he has used this tragedy to inspire thousands of people to truly do what they love & grab life with all your might and go for it!!!

I have known Ryan for a number of years and have witnessed his awe-inspiring growth. When you read this book, you will want to sort all your Sh*t by the time you have got half way through...

Ryan is an absolute savage when it comes to loving life, doing life & winning at life and helping others to do the same!!!

I believe this book will be one of your go-to manuals for the rest of your life."

Sir Marco Robinson:
#1 Bestselling Author
#2 Netflix producer
Entrepreneur of the Year
#1 Presenter & Creator of the prime-time TV Show, 'Get a house for free'

CONTENTS PAGE

SORT YOUR S-H-I-T OUT!

THIS BOOK ISN'T FOR PEOPLE...

Who want to buy a house, get married, have kids, and then die.

Who want to waste their time doing things they don't enjoy.

Who want to work in an unfulfilling job their whole life.

Who want to spend their time around negative people.

Who want to blame everyone else for their life.

Who enjoy constantly feeling unhappy.

Who aren't willing to make changes.

Who want to die with regrets.

WE DON'T GROW WHEN THINGS ARE EASY, WE GROW WHEN WE FACE CHALLENGES

Growing up throughout my teenage years I was extremely confused with what I wanted to do in life, to the point where I became extremely lost. I spent a great deal of my precious teenage time doing a variety of things that didn't add to my overall happiness, and I also spent a lot of time with groups of people who weren't on the same wavelength as me. Deep down I knew there was something different, something bigger, and something better for my life, but I just didn't know what that was back then, and I didn't have a fucking clue where to find it.

With absolutely no guidance from anyone around me, the lack of direction saw me as a pupil being pressured into picking a career path. I ended up choosing to learn how to become a car mechanic as I enjoyed riding motorbikes, so why wouldn't I enjoy fixing cars? The first few years were the 'golden years' of my career as everything I was doing was a completely new and exciting experience, and I was progressing on a daily basis.

On a night out in November 2011, as a scrawny 18-year-old boy, I was violently attacked whilst on the way home from a nightclub where I suffered from a fractured skull and a blood clot due to a bleed on the brain. I had to be put into a coma, and whilst in the coma on the life support machine doctors planned to pull the plug on me as I was considered completely brain dead, but thankfully for me my dad saved my life by telling the specialists, "NO FUCKING WAY," and I later went on to making a slow but full recovery over the coming weeks, months, and years.

After coming out of hospital I went back to catch up on and complete my three-year college apprenticeship scheme, but after becoming a fully qualified vehicle technician, the job satisfaction began to swiftly fade away. As I had now reached my qualification target, the work soon went from exciting to exhausting. Work went from the thrill of stripping a complete engine down over the course of a few days, to the bore of spending many mornings laying upside down in a cold, dark, and wet footwell trying to blindly undo a dashboard bolt with one hand.

Not long after my traumatic brain injury I found myself in a relationship for over 6 years, however, after it began to crumble in 2018, I sadly went on to seeing the person who I loved sat in a restaurant with another guy, and this was only just a few days before we had planned our trip to visit South Africa. And after returning from my first ever solo backpacking trip to Cape Town to what was now an empty home, the deep downhill spiral of depression really started to kick in.

After many months of mental misery, I managed to completely transform my mindset with the help of one single thought, which ended up leading me on to starting my own journey of self-discovery and becoming the very best version of myself. Over the next couple of years, I worked on myself every single day, started facing some of my greatest fears, and soon waved goodbye to my old life. I started surrounding myself with people who showed me my unique gifts and helped pull the magic out of me, and after being challenged by someone who I had only just met online in 2021, I ended up quitting my one and only, unfulfilling day job of over a decade, to pursue my newly found purpose. This was after realising that I had information stored within my mind which could be used to help guide many individuals up and out of the ditch they were currently stuck in, so that they could then embark on their own personal path of purpose.

I then spent many months and years looking for all the right answers in all the wrong places, and I also asked all the wrong questions to all the wrong people, but in doing so I found that there is no one set of specific answers for your life; what's right for me may be wrong for you and vice versa. However, after spending thousands of hours studying the greats and interviewing some of life's happiest, healthiest, and wealthiest individuals, I've found that there is a universal blueprint which is a set of foundations that can be used to inform and instruct you on how to create the life of your dreams.

This isn't just a book to read and then put back on your shelf gathering dust. This is a user manual that has been carefully created to help guide you from where you currently are to where you want to be with less stress, struggle, and suffering. At the end of each chapter there will be a 'chapter challenge', which will require you to take some uncomfortable action, but don't worry because I've created this to be challenging but not impossible.

So, let's make today the first day of your new and improved life!

"Growth is painful. Change is painful. But nothing is as painful as staying stuck somewhere you don't belong."

DEPRESSION TO PROGRESSION

The most difficult time of my life was when I was going through a long-term relationship breakup. When I tell people this, they are extremely surprised that I didn't say it was the time when I was lying there in a coma on my deathbed. Sure, that was a challenging time, but mainly for my loved ones. I wasn't actually conscious at the beginning, so when they wanted to pull the plug, my life was totally in somebody else's hands. But on the other hand, when I was suffering from depression, my life was in my very own hands, and at one point I almost opted to, 'pull the plug' on myself!

After seeing the woman I loved sat in a restaurant with another guy back in 2019, I ended up suffering through many months of mental misery as I was down and depressed, and it felt like my whole world had come crashing down. Every single day was like a Groundhog Day where I would wake up and do the same old S-H-I-T over and over again. I'd wake up and cry. I'd get dressed and cry. I'd drive to work and cry. I'd get to work and spend my whole day overthinking; it felt like negative thought after negative thought would compound on top of each other, and I couldn't ever stop it. Some days I'd completely break down and cry, and other days I'd get angry and lash out at things. I'd leave work and go home to cry, then once the week was over, I'd spend my weekends sat crying. The days that I decided to drag myself to the gym, I'd just sit on the machines and stare into space. It was such a weird feeling because I didn't actually want to be there, but I also didn't want to be sat at home alone either and, after a short period, I decided to just quit the gym completely. I was stuck in this vicious downhill spiral, feeling like I was trapped in a prison within my own home; at this point I was very lonely, confused, and desperate.

I'd spend my free time focusing all my energy on trying to understand why this had happened 'to me' and was constantly trying to think of ways in which I could alter the past. I would beat myself up mentally on a daily basis and tell myself all the reasons for why I would NEVER EVER be happy again. After a few months of going round in circles, things began to get a whole lot worse. I'd become extremely desperate and hated my own company; I hated the sound of silence, but that was all I had back then. At one point I was so desperate to find 'happiness' that I went through a stage of GOOGLE-ING, 'how to be happy' every single night whilst in bed. I would franticly scour the whole internet in hopes of discovering all the answers, and at one point I had become that determined, that I wouldn't even sleep at all some nights. I remember dragging myself multiple times through a day's work whilst running on empty. Those days I felt like a fucking zombie; I had literally completed the, 'how to be happy' level on the game of GOOGLE the night before, but still wasn't any happier. At this point I felt like giving up because I couldn't find happiness anywhere. Until the time where I thought that I had found the answers I was desperately looking for…
One weekend I decided to download a couple of social media apps and started looking at what everyone else was doing with their spare time. I suddenly saw the 'happiness' on other people's faces and confirmed to myself that I should start doing exactly what they were doing if I wanted to be as happy as they were. So I did. Overnight my weekends went from sat indoors crying my eyes out, to the polar opposite which was to go out to bars, pubs, and clubs. Before I knew it, I had become unhappy just drinking on

the weekends, so I started to drink within the week too. (This is the same person who would normally drink only just a handful of times per year, and now was drinking a handful of times per week, and sometimes even a handful of times per day). Sure, it felt good for a very short period of time, but only until I realised it wasn't making me feel that good at all, and it was actually making me feel worse. When I finally noticed this, I knew that I needed to change things up fast.

The night that completely turned things upside down... One weekend I was out on the town knocking back the bevvies and I realised that I was absolutely slaughtered. I could barely stand up, I couldn't hardly speak, and I just wanted to fall asleep. But only until I was introduced to cocaine for the very first time. I was offered some and was ensured that it would instantly make me feel much better. Before this evening I was always so anti-drug as I had seen the carnage that it can leave behind. Of course, I knew what it was, but I had never touched it before. But this night was different. I had nothing left to lose. So why wouldn't I give it a go?

So, I did. Within a matter of minutes this S-H-I-T had hit me. I went from falling asleep at the bar to busting some crazy-ass moves out on the dancefloor, and anyone that even dared to look at me for the slightest second would get pulled in to come and join me in my moment of madness. But within the hour I was on a downer and was then back outside for another top-up of nasal energy. After doing this a few times throughout the night, I was totally unaware of where I was or what I was doing. I remembered leaving the bar and that was it. Waking up later that Sunday morning gave me painful heart palpitations. I opened my eyes and thought, "WHERE THE FUCK AM I?" after realising that

I wasn't actually in my bed or even in my house. Lucky for me I soon found out I was at a friend's place. What a crazy night. WTF happened!? I just wanted to go home.

After returning back home everything came completely crashing down. I felt like absolute S-H-I-T, and I felt even worse than the days before. So yet again I went and curled up, crying in bed. I didn't shower or eat that evening, and just laid waiting for Monday to come round before forcing myself up and out to work to go and do it all over again. At this point in time not only was my mental and physical health suffering, but so was my personal hygiene. I felt disgusting but didn't know what I could or should do to change this feeling. I absolutely hated myself.

As the weeks went by, you'd find me constantly scanning social media to see who was out and about, and who wanted to go for drinks. Then once the weekends came round, I'd be in and out of different pubs and clubs whilst back on the packet. It got to a point where I didn't even care if anyone I knew was out or not, I'd just rock up and get pissed, then chat to anyone and everyone. Those weeks quickly turned into months and every single Sunday without fail I'd be sat there at home crying my eyes out knowing full well that I was stuck on this awful roundabout, but not knowing when I should get off, or indeed if I could ever get off. I was trapped in this cycle of S-H-I-T and didn't know what to do about it. At this moment in time death for me was in fact a desired destination. I would now wake up in the mornings and shout the words, "FUCK YOU!" because I was so gutted to wake up and was so pissed off that I had to face yet another day of despair.

I was keeping all this S-H-I-T bottled up to myself for months and had so many thoughts rushing round in my head that I didn't even know what to do. I had complete brain fog where I had thought after thought piling up on top of each other. I started to think maybe it would be better to just call it a day, but as much as I really didn't want to wake up most mornings, I also had a huge fear of death. It was weird. It was like I didn't want to live any more, but I also really didn't want to die. I didn't know what the right answer was, but what I did know is that suicide felt like my only option because I couldn't go on like this anymore...

Things got so bad that I ended up booking myself an appointment to go and see a doctor at my local GP. I remember leaving work around midday to drive over, and as I was driving, I was thinking, "What am I going to say?" and "I wonder if she'll understand me?" I was so nervous. I arrived and then sat staring at the brick wall in the dingy waiting room whilst waiting for my name to be called. "Ryan Nurse" – I was up. I walked into the small room and sat in front of a doctor who I had never met before, and I instantly felt her energy. It seemed like she was running behind a little. She asked me why I was visiting, and I just started to unload everything which was all bottled up inside of me waiting to come bursting out. After about a minute of me pouring my heart out, I was suddenly stopped in my tracks. It felt like she didn't want to listen to me, and it seemed like she was so quick to push the prescription across the desk to say, "You are depressed." I was told I needed to go through this course of antidepressants and that they would hopefully make me feel better, but before feeling any better I would first feel a lot worse. This petrified me as I already thought that I had hit rock bottom, and I didn't know how much worse I could feel before I did something which my future self would have really regretted. She also told me I didn't have to take them if I didn't want to, so I should go away and think about it. THANKS! The person who can't make decisions now has another thing to add to the list of all the other S-H-I-T that was tumbling around in my washing machine of a mind. Now with the ball back in my court, I drove back to work with the prescription sat on the passenger seat staring at me. Did I want to take antidepressants? What will happen to me if I feel any worse than I feel right now? I just wanted all this S-H-I-T to be over!

After returning to work I had a conversation with my manager about whether I should get the antidepressants and take them or not, and also spoke to my parents briefly that evening too. A few days went by where I was just thinking about it and had gotten nowhere. I thought there must be another option as I believed I hadn't yet exhausted all avenues, so I was determined to try something other than taking the tablets; I booked myself back in for another appointment at the doctors. I managed to get an appointment for the next week and after another alcohol and cocaine fuelled weekend, I found myself back in that same waiting room staring at that same wall once more. I was called back in to see the same doctor for the second time. I walked in and sat down then literally told her that I was so scared to take the antidepressants as I believed that if I felt any worse, I would end up taking my life. She just stared at me. So I pleaded with her. "There must be another option," "Is there not somebody who I can just talk to?" and that's when she gave me the option to try Cognitive Behaviour Therapy (CBT).

She told me I had to be put on the waiting list which would take a few weeks, but I actually felt better for a brief moment as I now had something which I could focus on and look forward to. A few extremely challenging weeks went by before it was time for my first CBT call. I was offered to do these in person, but I decided not to as it would mean leaving work early for a number of weeks and I felt that was bad for the company. So, I decided to do over the phone sessions sat in my car which had no A/C whilst the windows were all the way up. This was so no one else could hear, and this was right in the middle of the red-hot summer heat. It was like being sat in a sauna, but anyway, after a few sessions, things were going ok, but then after a few more it felt as though everything was so scripted. Every time I deviated off track I was pulled back to the script and didn't get the chance to just get things off my chest. I suddenly started feeling worse after each call so decided to lie my way out of this. One lunch time I told the young lady that I was miraculously feeling better than ever before and that I didn't need any further sessions. That same weekend I prepared to take my own life.

That Saturday I was sat sprawled out on the sofa whilst sobbing as usual. I had all these horrible thoughts bouncing around my brain about how I would never be happy again, and how I'd be better off dead. I knew exactly what I was going to do but was just too scared to go ahead with it. I had the classic shoulder angel in one ear and the shoulder devil in the other. That little fucker was prodding me saying, "Go on, do it, don't be a pussy," and the angel was constantly reminding me that my biggest fear was death, and how I would leave absolute carnage behind if I was to go through with it. I really didn't know what to do, so I did nothing. I just sat there in silence with tears streaming down my face, and in that moment, I felt absolutely worthless because I couldn't even make my fucking mind up whether to die or not. I already felt as if I couldn't do anything right, and this just confirmed it to me as I couldn't even kill myself properly.

Suddenly out of nowhere a thought came into my mind and I held on to it so tight; I had the feeling of being magnetized towards it. That thought said, "Could I live with the thought of dying with regrets." So I asked myself that question... Could I live with the thought of dying with regrets? I asked it again, and again, and again. Could I live knowing full well that I hadn't even really tried to pull myself up and out of the ditch that I had dug for myself? The answer was NO! For all these months I had been hoping that someone else was going to come and 'set me free' but the reality was that the only person who could have set me free, was me. I started to look back on my life and all the S-H-I-T I had already overcome. There and then in that very moment it was if a huge transition had shifted within my mind. I realised that I had been focusing on all the negative things, so instead I started to look around me at all of the positive things which I currently had. I had a roof over my head, I had food in my fridge, I had clothes on my back, and I had shoes on my feet. I then realised that the nightmare I thought I was going through was in fact a dream for somebody else. Because there were so many people out there living on that cold hard concrete, wishing they could have traded places with me. I realised that I had been focusing on all of my perceived problems and in return I was just attracting more of them towards me. Because in life you get more of what it is that you focus on.

After that thought I felt the urge to write, so I did. I started to write down all the thoughts that had been bouncing around in my brain, and I instantly felt a huge relief of pressure from within my mind. It was crazy! Why hadn't I thought of writing things down before? I could now clearly see everything that I was frantically trying to untangle inside my skull, and in all honesty seeing it there in front of me, written down on a piece of paper, made it look not that bad at all. For months I had created a story in my head, and I'd begun to believe all the S-H-I-T which I was telling myself. I had felt that I was trapped within this prison for so long, but the only prison we are ever trapped in is the one that we have made within our own minds. Because your mind can either be your best friend or your own worst enemy. Just know that thoughts do become things, and what you think about you'll bring about. Focus on what you do want rather than what you don't want, because whatever you do decide to focus on will increase. Of course, you can't always choose your first thought, but you can always choose your second, and the great thing about this is that if you change your thinking, you can literally change your life. Remember that your perception will shape your reality, because if you think life is S-H-I-T then it is, but if you think life is great then it also is. You may have heard of the term, 'the law of attraction' which states that positive thoughts generate positive feelings and in return will attract positive life experiences, but don't forget that the exact same applies for the negative ones too.

That evening before I went to bed, I wrote down all the things I was thankful to have in my life. It felt so good that I did it the next evening too, and then I started doing it both morning and night. Twice a day I would now write a gratitude list, and in all honesty, I didn't even know what the word gratitude meant back then, but it was working. Before I knew it, I had replaced the "FUCK YOU," with "THANK YOU," after realising how precious this priceless gift of life really is. I realised that we all open two gifts every single day, and that is our eyes; and that's why they call this moment the present. I now believe that gratitude is the gateway key to a life of abundance, because each day that I wrote down the things which I was thankful for, I would then feel that little bit better inside, and after a short period I began to attract more of the good things towards me. If you can't be grateful for the small things that come into your life, then what makes you think you'll ever be grateful for the big things that may come into your life? And if you're not grateful for what you have in your life already, then what the fuck makes you think that you're going to be grateful when you've got more? Just realise, that true happiness isn't getting what you want, but it's wanting what you've already got, and gratitude makes certain that what you have is enough. You can never be angry and grateful at the exact same time, so from then on, I stopped counting my problems and started counting my blessings.

I stopped looking at what I thought I was 'losing' and focused on everything which I was potentially gaining. Back then, all I had focused on was losing my house and losing my girlfriend. However, I later realised that the worst things that happen in your life can also turn out to become the very best things; sometimes your most profound periods of pain can also turn out to be your greatest gifts of growth. Again, I made the conscious decision to shift my mindset to look at all the future potential opportunities I had and realised that I now had a fresh blank page to paint on and start designing the life of my dreams.

Anytime you feel that you've hit rock bottom in your life, just tell yourself that it's actually a good place to be, because the only way from there is up! If you ever feel like you have, 'nothing left to lose', then flip your thinking to realise that you now have, 'everything left to gain'. Sometimes in life you have to lose yourself to then find yourself. You have break 'you' in order to remake 'you', but this time into the person who you wish you'd been all along. Stop focusing all of your energy on trying to repair the old and start focusing on building the new.

Life is a journey that's full of many priceless hidden lessons and for months I was living each day with the victim mentality of, "Why is this happening TO me," instead of shifting my thoughts to a more growth minded way of thinking which was to ask myself, "Why is this happening FOR me?" I began to see that these painful events were in fact all happening in my favour. I didn't see it in the moment but now looking back from an experienced set of eyes, I can tell you that these painful events turned out to become some of the greatest gifts of my life.

When I was going through those tough times in my life, I believed it would be better to bottle up all those thoughts, feelings, and emotions. However, I later realised that it was actually the worst thing I could have done, and by doing so it made things that much worse over time. Reaching out for help is sometimes super scary but believe me when I say that this is what's going get you from where you currently are to where you want to be much quicker than by trying to figure all the S-H-I-T out yourself within your own mind.

15

Know that vulnerability is a superpower, and when you can become vulnerable yourself, this is actually when the true healing happens. By opening your heart and sharing your light with the world, not only do you begin to heal yourself even more, but your light is used to then help guide others up and out of the dark place that they are currently in and into the light. It shows others that it's safe to do so, and it also gives them the permission to do the same. Because vulnerability is the key to connection.

If you find yourself in a real S-H-I-T situation similar to the ones that I went through, I am telling you to never give up on yourself because you are so worth working on. Even if you don't feel like it right now, I want to remind you that you are amazing just the way you are, and that you can still become so much more. So don't ever suffer in silence; reach out to someone, because there are so many people out there who will want to help you. As long as you still have breath in your lungs then you can take the required steps to turn your life around. Please believe me when I say that suicide is a permanent solution to a temporary problem, and you should never make a permanent decision based on a temporary feeling in any area of your life. Because when emotion is high logic is low.

"Life is our greatest lesson and loss is our greatest teacher."

WHAT DID I LEARN FROM THIS AND HOW CAN IT HELP YOU?

BELOW I HAVE LISTED SOME OF THE MOST IMPORTANT LESSONS I LEARNED FROM THIS DIFFICULT PERIOD OF MY LIFE WHICH INCLUDE:
- Your perception will shape your reality.
- You can't control other people's thoughts, opinions, words, or actions.
- If nothing changes, then nothing changes.
- What you focus on expands.
- Self-talk is vital to live a truly happy life.
- True happiness is homemade.
- Nobody is coming. You must save yourself.
- Comparison is the thief of joy.
- Avoiding your problems won't fix them.
- Love yourself first and become your own best friend.
- Your surroundings shape you.
- Vulnerability is a superpower.
- Don't bottle things up, and always ask for help.
- Suicide isn't the only way out of your mess.
- It only takes one thing to completely change your life.
- Gratitude is everything and more.
- Progress equals happiness.
- You'll never think your way out of overthinking.
- Thoughts really do become things.
- Life is always happening in your favour.
- You get to choose how you feel in any given moment.
- There is a lesson in every situation.
- Life is the greatest gift you'll ever receive.

When we are at the centre of these S-H-I-T storms it's easy to confuse ourselves into believing that there is no way out and that we are going to be trapped forever. That's why I want to share my journey with you so that you don't have to try and battle through this somewhat challenging era of your life alone. Throughout this book I will explain more about these difficulties in further detail, and also teach you how you can use these tools to your advantage to begin building a better future. Sometimes in life you don't really realise your own strength until you come face to face with your greatest weakness. This is because you never know how strong you really are until being strong is your only option.

WHERE TO START?

I know what it's like to feel a little lost in life, where you really want to change your life for the better but are clueless on where to begin. You have so many thoughts rattling around in your mind that you become overwhelmed and don't end up doing anything at all. These thoughts build on top of each other and then the only thing you achieve is to stress yourself out and beat yourself up for not taking any action. It can feel as if you are stuck on a roundabout going round and round but don't know when to get off. As obvious as this sounds, if you want to start something new you MUST start at the start! So, if you're currently feeling lost in life then look at this as a good thing, because you are aware that there is so much more to be found, and now it's time for you to discover what you really want and need in your life.

Look I'm not going to BS you into believing you can completely change your life overnight, because that isn't the case at all. However, you can start today by coming up with a clear vision of exactly what you want, to create a transition plan for the future, and to then evolve into the new and improved version of yourself to become that person and eventually live your dream life.

So many people think they are going to take one giant step from their current reality to some sort of 'insta famous lifestyle' without first setting the solid foundations which are vital to start building a better future for themselves. Just imagine if the world's tallest building (which is currently the Burj Khalifa in Dubai standing just over half a mile tall at 829.8 meters) was built on a set of S-H-I-T foundations. What do you think would happen to it when mother nature blows her almighty gusts of wind? It's the same for you in any area of your life. If you want to begin building a fantastic life for yourself but aren't willing to first construct the solid foundations, then things could all seem fine, but one-day out of nowhere... BOOM! Everything comes crashing down with little to no warning. So that's why it's so essential for you to get your S-H-I-T together. Then you'll be more likely to weather any storms that may come your way in life.

The first step is to start afresh by getting all those thoughts out of your head and putting them on to paper. This way you can actually see what you're dealing with, and you will also give yourself some well needed thinking space to then create solutions rather than just more perceived problems. Trust me when I say that you'll never think your way out of overthinking, because overthinking is the art of creating problems that don't even exist. This is why you MUST use your journal rather than trying to untangle the mess within your mind. Your skull is solid and can only hold a certain number of thoughts before the pressure becomes too much and you then become overwhelmed, and that's the reason why you need to literally think on paper. Getting everything out on paper is going to help you stop MAGNIFYING your problems to look much bigger than what they actually are. Just because one area of your life is currently crap, it doesn't mean that your whole life is S-H-I-T.

CHAPTER CHALLENGE

This challenge requires you to be TOTALLY honest with yourself and take out your journal, sit somewhere quiet, have no distractions, and just start writing. Use this task to clear some space in your head by unloading all the S-H-I-T you've got going on up in there. This is a great way of assessing where you currently are, seeing what you're currently constantly thinking about, and also understanding the reason/s for why you want to start this journey.

IF YOU NEED SOME HELP, THEN HERE ARE A FEW QUESTIONS YOU COULD ASK YOURSELF TO GET STARTED:

1. **How would I describe my current life in 3 words?**
2. **What do I think about the most each day?**
3. **What is the biggest challenge in my life right now?**
4. **What would I like to change in my life?**
5. **Why do I want to change that?**
6. **What has stopped me from changing this already?**

"You're only as solid as the foundations you build on."

AWARENESS IS EVERYTHING

The first phase of changing anything in your life begins with awareness, because you can't change something that you don't know needs changing. It's awareness that gives you choices, and it's choices that ultimately give you freedom. Awareness allows you to be present in the moment and to be fully engaged in what's going on in your life. Awareness can lead to several benefits including the ability to make better decisions, to help improve relationships, and can help you identify and overcome any limiting beliefs, patterns, and/or habits. Also being aware of your own thoughts, emotions, and actions can equally lead to improved mental health and overall well-being.

TYPES OF AWARENESS:
1. **Self-awareness:** This can help you understand, regulate, and manage your own thoughts, emotions, and behaviours which can lead to increased personal growth and development.
2. **Environmental Awareness:** This can help you understand and appreciate the world around you, and then make informed decisions about how you interact with the environment.
3. **Social Awareness:** This can help you understand and empathize with others, which can lead to improved communication and stronger relationships.
4. **Cultural Awareness:** This can help you understand and respect the diversity of cultures, to then make considerate decisions about how you interact with people from different backgrounds.
5. **Mental and Physical Awareness:** This can help you identify and address any issues that may be

affecting your overall health and well-being, which can further lead you on to living a better quality of life.

6. **Awareness of One's Own Bias:** This can help you make more educated and fairer decisions, which can lead you to becoming more understanding and open-minded.

Change always starts with self, because when things change inside you, things change around you. Self-awareness is the ability to know and understand one's own thoughts, feelings, and actions and how they may affect others. It's having the ability to reflect on your own mental states and processes, and to recognise yourself as an individual who's totally separate from others and the environment around you. Having good self-awareness is considered a key part of human consciousness and personal development.

Self-awareness is a practice that must be developed over time and for many it can be a very uncomfortable thing to do, but if you're not willing to look in the mirror at yourself to learn more about who you are as a person, and by not being aware of your own thoughts, emotions, and actions you could end up unintentionally hurting somebody else, or even hurting yourself. Self-awareness allows us to question ourselves before reacting to certain situations, to be more open-minded to other people's thoughts, views, and opinions, and to learn more about ourselves and the people around us.

WAYS IN WHICH YOU CAN PRACTICE SELF-AWARENESS:

1. **Mindfulness Meditation:** Sit somewhere comfortable and quiet, close your eyes, and focus on your breath. Be the observer of your thoughts and emotions without any judgement and let them pass through your mind just like the clouds in the sky.

2. **Journaling:** Write down all your thoughts, feelings, and experiences on a daily basis. Reflect on what you have written and over time look for repeated patterns or themes in your behaviours.

3. **Self-reflection:** Set aside some time each week to reflect on what's happened, what you've learned, and how it can help you grow. Realise that just because you may have had a S-H-I-T day or two doesn't mean you've had a S-H-I-T life!

4. **Feedback From Others:** Ask a best friend, family member, or someone you trust to give you their honest perspective on your behaviour and ask them how you come across to others.

5. **Self-compassion:** Be kind and understanding towards yourself instead of criticising and beating yourself up mentally.

6. **Learn From Your Mistakes:** Accept responsibility for your actions and reflect on what you could possibly do different next time.

It's also very important to be aware of your emotions as your emotions are the reporters for the soul. It is vital that you notice and feel all your emotions, whatever type of emotion they may be. If you're happy then feel happy, but if you're sad then feel sad, because for some reason when we feel S-H-I-T, we as humans still feel the need to change that and always be happy. Just realise that if you hold on to negative emotions without feeling or releasing them, then they will stay inside you and manifest into much greater things in the future until you do. This is because unexpressed emotions will never die, they are buried alive and will come forth later in much uglier ways. Repressed emotions refer to emotions that you unconsciously avoid, and supressed emotions are entirely voluntarily. Realise that all emotions need to be expressed to be processed, because any trapped negative emotions will get in your way, they will sabotage your efforts to create the life of your dreams and will also make you pretty miserable along the way. Suppression can sometimes be a good short-term solution, but repressed emotions might show up later as a range of different physical or even psychological symptoms. Overall, both repression and suppression involve the management of emotions, but repression occurs on an unconscious level, while suppression on the other hand is a conscious act. Repressed emotions remain hidden in the unconscious mind, potentially impacting one's mental well-being, while suppressed emotions involve conscious control over the expression or experience of emotions.

BELOW IS SOME MORE INFORMATION ABOUT BOTH REPRESSED AND SUPPRESSED EMOTIONS:
1. **Repressed Emotions:** Repressed emotions refer to the unconscious act of pushing distressing or uncomfortable emotions, thoughts, or memories out of one's conscious awareness. This defence mechanism is believed to occur as a means of coping with overwhelming or traumatic experiences. When a person represses emotions,

they avoid consciously acknowledging or experiencing them.

KEY FEATURES OF REPRESSED EMOTIONS INCLUDE:

a. **Unconscious Process:** Repression operates on an unconscious level, meaning individuals are often unaware that they are repressing their emotions. The emotions are pushed into the unconscious mind, making them inaccessible to conscious awareness.

b. **Involuntary Nature:** Repression typically happens automatically and involuntarily. It is a mechanism employed by the mind to shield the individual from emotional pain or discomfort.

c. **Potential for Resurfacing:** Repressed emotions can resurface in various ways, such as through dreams, slips of the tongue, or triggered emotional reactions. These emotions may manifest indirectly or through related symptoms, impacting one's mental and physical well-being.

d. **Psychological Impact:** If repressed emotions are not addressed or resolved, they may contribute to psychological distress, such as anxiety, depression, or relationship difficulties. Unresolved trauma or repressed emotions can also interfere with personal growth and hinder emotional healing.

2. **Suppressed Emotions:** Suppressed emotions, on the other hand, involve a conscious effort to control or inhibit one's emotional expressions or experiences. When someone suppresses emotions, they are aware of their emotional state but choose not to express or fully experience those emotions.

KEY FEATURES OF SUPPRESSED EMOTIONS INCLUDE:

a. **Conscious Process:** Suppression is a deliberate and conscious act of holding back or controlling emotions. Individuals actively decide not to express or fully experience their emotions due to various reasons, such as social norms, personal beliefs, or situational considerations.

b. **Voluntary Control:** Unlike repression, suppression requires voluntary control and conscious effort to manage emotions. It involves restraining the outward expression of emotions without necessarily addressing the underlying emotional experiences.

c. **Temporary Nature:** Suppressed emotions tend to be temporary, and individuals may release or express them at a more appropriate time or place. The emotions are not permanently buried in the unconscious but consciously regulated for a specific period.

d. **Potential Consequences:** While suppressing emotions in certain situations can be adaptive and socially appropriate, chronic or excessive suppression can have adverse effects. It may lead to emotional numbness, increased stress, difficulties in interpersonal relationships, and potential long-term psychological consequences.

Understand that emotions play an important role in how you think, feel, and behave, and the emotions you do feel each day can either compel you to take actions and steps forwards, or can stall your progress in making the important moves in your life. With any negative emotion you have, you must feel it to heal it. We are only humans at the end of the day, so if you're sad then feel sad. It's ok to feel upset, pissed off, and to cry it out from time to time, but don't ever confuse FACTS with thoughts and feelings.

So, with this being said, any time you do feel these types of emotions, I want you to use something which is called the 5-minute rule. Set your phone timer for 5 minutes and allow yourself to scream, shout, kick, cry. You can even lay on your bed and beat the S-H-I-T out of your pillow if you have to, but just do whatever you need (as long as it doesn't hurt others) to get all of those built-up emotions out of your body. Once those five minutes are up then take in a huge deep breath and move on with your life. Because if it isn't going to matter in 5 years' time then why would you spend more than 5 minutes of your priceless time upset, annoyed, or worrying about it? Learn to let go of any unwanted emotions because those blockages that are trapped in your body will drain your energy and eventually lead to burnout, emotional imbalance, and possibly disease. Unresolved emotions stuck inside you are lying dormant and will eventually start to fester, build, and ultimately burst. So, whenever you don't feel great, feel the feeling but don't *become* the emotion. Witness it, allow it, and then release it.

CHAPTER CHALLENGE
When you feel negative emotions, asking yourself certain questions can help you gain insight, understand your emotions better, and find ways to cope effectively. This challenge is going to have you question yourself next time you notice you are getting angry or upset with someone or something. When this happens next it's time to take out your journal and answer these questions:

1. **What am I feeling right now?** – Identifying and labelling the specific emotion(s) you're experiencing can help you acknowledge and validate your feelings.
2. **Why am I feeling this way?** – Reflection on the possible triggers or underlying reasons for your negative emotions. Consider both external factors (events, situations, interactions) and the internal factors (thoughts, beliefs, memories) that might be contributing to your emotional state.
3. **Is there a pattern to these emotions?** – Be curious and explore whether there is a recurring pattern or specific circumstances that tend to evoke similar negative emotions. Recognizing patterns can provide clues about potential triggers or unresolved issues.
4. **Am I interpreting the situation accurately?** – Assess the thoughts and assumptions that accompany your negative emotions. Are you making any cognitive distortions, jumping to conclusions, or engaging in black-and-white thinking? Challenging and reframing your interpretations can help shift your perspective.
5. **How can I take care of myself in this moment?** – Consider self-care strategies that can help you manage your negative emotions effectively. This might include activities like engaging in hobbies, practicing mindfulness or relaxation techniques, seeking support from loved ones, or engaging in physical exercise.
6. **What can I learn from this emotional experience?** – Negative emotions often carry valuable information about our needs, values, and

boundaries. Reflect on what lessons or insights you can gain from this experience.

7. **What are some healthy ways I can express or process these emotions?** – Explore healthy outlets for expressing or processing your emotions. This could involve talking to a trusted friend or therapist, writing in a journal, engaging in creative outlets like art or music, or engaging in physical activities that allow you to release pent-up emotions, like going to the gym.

8. **Are there any potential solutions or actions I can take?** – If the negative emotions are stemming from a specific problem or situation, consider brainstorming potential solutions or actions you can take to address the issue. Taking proactive steps can help you regain a sense of control and empowerment.

9. **Can I practice self-compassion?** – Offer yourself kindness and understanding during challenging emotional moments. Treat yourself with the same compassion you would extend to a friend going through a difficult time.

Remember that these questions serve as a starting point for self-reflection and exploration. Everyone's experiences are unique, so adapt the questions to suit your specific circumstance and needs.

BELOW ARE SOME BONUS QUESTIONS YOU COULD ALSO ASK AND ANSWER YOURSELF:

10. **How do my past experiences shape my present perspective and behaviour?**
11. **How do my current thoughts and emotions influence my actions?**
12. **What are my core values and how do they influence my decisions?**
13. **What upsets me most about other people's behaviour?**
14. **What impact do my words and actions have on other people?**
15. **How would I feel if I was on the receiving end?**
16. **What are my strengths and weaknesses, and how can I work on improving them?**

Know that negative attracts negative, just as positive attracts positive, and when you start to feel good inside, it radiates and starts to attract the good around you. Because whatever you achieve inwardly will change your outer reality.

"Awareness is the greatest agent for change."

START WHERE YOU ARE

It's now time to really evaluate yourself. Since you're reading this book, I'm more than confident in saying that you're not 100% satisfied in every area of your life right now, and you know that you are currently seeking change. This is great news. You should be proud, happy, and excited, because now you have the awareness that there is so much more for you to achieve and become, and you can now start to create the action steps required to begin making your desired improvements. This begins by honestly assessing where you currently are in all areas of your life without any judgements. Assessing yourself is not only necessary for change but is also regularly required to maintain optimum standards for your life; you will never master what you don't measure, and you can never address the things you don't assess.

Understand that no problem is permanent or personal. It's so easy to get stuck in a self-pity-party thinking that life is chucking all the crap only in your direction, making you believe that there is something really wrong with you. You start to convince yourself that you aren't good enough, smart enough, or beautiful enough. Know that whatever S-H-I-T is going on in your life right now, it can be changed just as long as you decide that you want to change, and that you are willing to put in the work required to make the change. Believe me when I say that there is also someone else going through the same thing, and there is also someone who has just got through to the other side, so this proves that you are not alone in this S-H-I-T storm, and that there is a definitely a way of getting out the other end.

SOME OF THE BENEFITS OF ASSESSING YOUR LIFE INCLUDE:

1. **Clarity on Goals and Priorities:** By taking stock of where you currently are in your life, you can gain a better understanding of what you want to achieve, and what is most important to you right now.

2. **Increased Self-awareness:** Assessing your life can help you understand your strengths, weaknesses, values, and motivations, which can lead to greater self-awareness and personal growth.

3. **Improved Decision-making:** When you understand yourself more, you are aware of your goals and priorities, and are now better equipped to make clearer decisions that align with them.

4. **Greater Satisfaction:** By regularly assessing your life, you can identify any areas that may need improvements and then take the required steps to address them, which in return can lead to greater overall fulfilment.

5. **Sense of Direction:** Assessing your life can help you discover a sense of direction and purpose, which are essential to live a meaningful life.

6. **Better Mental and Emotional Well-being:** Reflecting on your life can help reduce stress, anxiety, and mental illness.

7. **Improved relationships:** Assessing your life can help you identify any patterns in your relationships with others that may be harmful for both you and them, and then make the required changes.

CHAPTER CHALLENGE

This challenge involves evaluating where you currently are in specific areas of your life, so you can see exactly what you need to focus on, and then are able to start making the desired improvements.

PERSONAL SELF-ASSESSMENT:
1. **Physical Health (10 points possible)**
2. **Mental Health (10 points possible)**
3. **Relationships (10 points possible)**
4. **Career/Work (10 points possible)**
5. **Finances (10 points possible)**
6. **Personal Growth and Development (10 points possible)**
7. **Spirituality/Religion (10 points possible)**
8. **Leisure and Hobbies (10 points possible)**

INSTRUCTIONS:
1. **For each area, rate yourself on a scale of 1-10, with 1 being the lowest and 10 being the highest.**
2. **Be totally honest with yourself and consider how you truly feel about each area.**
3. **Once you have completed the assessment, use the scores to identify areas where you may want to focus on improvement.**
4. **Start by doing a weekly check-in with yourself to look for any changes, patterns, or triggers that explain why the results may be different.**

Physical Health: _____
Mental Health: _____
Relationships: _____
Career/Work: _____
Finances: _____
Personal Growth and Development: _____
Spirituality/Religion: _____
Leisure/Hobbies: _____

TOTAL POSSIBLE SCORE: **80**
YOUR TOTAL SCORE: _____

You also need to learn to accept yourself for exactly who you are in this very moment so that you can eventually evolve into the very best version of yourself. Know that self-love and self-acceptance come from your childhood; some of us may have questioned our mother or father's love as very young children. Whenever we might have done something that wasn't 'right' in society's eyes we would have been told off or punished, and in return this may have made us believe that we weren't loved or good enough. At that innocent age if you did something that 'isn't right' then surely this means that you as a person are 'wrong?' Of course this isn't true, but our baby brains didn't understand this at the time, so now you need to realise that you've always been loved, and you've always been good enough. You are enough today, you were enough yesterday, and you will be enough tomorrow. You are whole and complete just the way you are, and you can still become much more than who you already are. Learn to accept yourself with no judgement for exactly who you are so you can then give yourself permission to work on yourself and in return love yourself so much more.

"You can't improve what you don't measure."

ACCEPT WHERE YOU ARE

It doesn't matter what's happened in your past because what's done is done. What matters is accepting the things that have happened, accepting where you currently are, and then creating the desired and required steps to get you to where you ultimately want to be in the future. Understand that you cannot change the past and the future is uncertain, but you can take control of your thoughts and actions in this present moment to help you grow as a person, and then you can create a better future for yourself and the people around you. As much as you would have liked certain things to have gone certain ways, you must accept that some things in life are totally out of your control, so accept them for what they are and focus on bettering yourself moving forwards. In life you can't control all situations, and you can't control other people's thoughts, opinions, words, or actions, but you can however control the meaning and the response that you give to them.

Understand that no amount of guilt can change the past, and no amount of worrying can change the future. There is nothing you can do to change the past, but you can certainly use those priceless lessons to improve your future. Overthinking about the future and focusing on the past is a way of ignoring the only moment you are guaranteed... which is this precious, present moment. I believe there is a positive which can be extracted from every negative situation in life, but it's down to you and you alone to discover these positives, and then use them to your advantage. Challenge yourself to start looking for the lessons in every adversity and not the losses. Sometimes it requires you to take a step back in order to have a different point of view; you can't read the label from inside the jar.

WAYS TO HELP YOU ACCEPT YOUR CURRENT
REALITY:
1. **Acknowledge and accept the reality of the situation:** It's super important to understand that resistance or denial of where you currently are will only prolong your suffering.
2. **Be mindful of your thoughts and emotions**: Recognise any negative or unhelpful thoughts and try to reframe them in a more positive light.
3. **Practice gratitude:** Be grateful for what you do have, rather than focusing on everything that you don't have.
4. **Focus on what you can control:** Control the controllables and forget the things you can't; you can then take the required actions to improve that specific situation.
5. **Journal:** Think on paper and get all those thoughts out of your head and onto somewhere that you can see them for what they really are.
6. **Practice Mindfulness:** Meditation, yoga, and walking are some great ways of calming your mind and bringing you back to this present moment.
7. **Mindset Shift:** Try to shift your perspective and look for all the positive aspects of your current situation.

Remember, accepting your current situation doesn't mean you have to like it, but it can help you move forwards in a more positive way. Acceptance is a process which takes time and effort, so be kind to yourself and give yourself the time and space you need to work through it, and also understand that how you look at the issue *is* the issue. It's not what happens to us that usually hurts us, but it's the meaning and the response that we give to those specific situations. Realise that it's your perception that will shape your reality, and just know that if you can change your thinking about those events, you can literally change your life; if you change the way you look at things, the things you look at change. Work to flip your mindset to start looking at every set-back as a set-up for an even greater come-back. A setback may put you on a more difficult path momentarily, but quite often will end up eventually leading you to an even better destination.

CHAPTER CHALLENGE

This challenge requires you to answer a set of questions in your journal to help pull some positives from your perceived negative past experiences. Start by writing down 1 – 5 of your past/present most difficult problems/challenges/events and then individually answer these questions for each:

1. **What are my thoughts and feelings about this situation?**
2. **What are the FACTS of this situation?**
3. **What are the potential benefits of this situation?**
4. **What could/can I control in this situation?**
5. **How could/can I take action to improve this situation?**
6. **What are the things I am grateful for from this situation?**
7. **How can I reframe my perspective on this situation?**
8. **What are the potential opportunities from this this situation?**
9. **What are the benefits of both accepting or resisting this situation?**
10. **How can I move forward in a more productive and healthier way?**

Sometimes you just have to make peace with your past in order to keep your future from becoming a constant battle. Learn to accept your past, embrace your present, and then plan for your future.

"You can't go back and change the beginning, but you can start where you are and change the ending."

S-H-I-T HAPPENS

At one point or another throughout life, you will find yourself at the centre of a S-H-I-T storm. Just know that you're not the only one, and if you think you're getting out the other side squeaky-clean then you best think again!

From facing and overcoming many different adversities throughout my life (all the way from deathbed to depression) I have discovered that this beautiful journey of life isn't always sunshine and rainbows and is more like S-H-I-T storms and EGOs. Believe me when I say that NOBODY is getting through this life without coming head-on with at least one majorly shitty situation. In life pain is inevitable but suffering on the other hand is optional. You can either be a victim or a victor of your past, and if you are still suffering today, then you my friend are a volunteer.

Know that pain speaks volumes, and it can be very beneficial to you if you choose to listen to what it's trying to tell you. This is because usually it is a messenger trying to tell you that what you are currently doing isn't quite right. Just imagine that you put your hand in a fire, what's going to happen? You would feel that pain as a physical sensation because it would burn your hand and it would fucking hurt. It's the same in your life. If you're doing something and it's causing you constant pain, then that's the messenger trying to tell you that you need to stop doing what you're currently doing and change something up, possibly have a different approach, or try something new. Listen to that pain and make that change!

Whatever happens to you in life may not be your fault, but whatever happens after is 100% your choice. You get to choose whether you react or respond to certain situations, and you get to choose whether you become bitter or better, but whatever it is that you decide to do will ultimately shape your future. So please realise that reaction creates captivity, however true freedom lies within a thoughtful response. You have to learn to master your emotions and take a moment to think before you reply, because the person who can remain calm in any situation always wins. Remember from the last chapter that it's not usually what happens to us that hurts us, but it's the meaning we give to that specific event. Your perception will always shape your reality; remember, how you look at the issue *becomes* the issue, but if you can change the meaning, you can literally change your life. So next time you find yourself in a real S-H-I-T situation just stop for a moment, take a breath, gather your thoughts, and then reply and respond rather than react and regret. There is so much power in the pause as it gives you the well-needed time to look for the positives that can be extracted from that situation, rather than focusing on all the negatives. Remember that whatever you focus on in life expands and you'll end up attracting more of that into your life. Take responsibility for your actions after any challenging event in your life, knowing that the word 'responsibility' actually means 'response' and 'ability'. You have the ability to respond, which in return allows you to extract the best out of any S-H-I-T situation. Learn to absorb the information, think, and then reply rather than rage, react, and feel remorse.

I honestly believe there is positive which can be extracted from every negative in life and that adversity can quite often turn out to be a blessing in disguise. From my own experience I have found that adversity is the prerequisite to growth, success, and true happiness. I believe that hidden at the very core of adversity is the key to progress and life-long happiness. It isn't going to be easy to find this key, but once you have obtained it, it will unlock the barrier to your next level of life. Whatever you do, make sure you focus on the good S-H-I-T because adversity can be a gift, but only if you choose to let it be. For instance, if someone says or does something that 'triggers' you, don't get upset or angry with that person, but thank them within your own mind as they have just taught you a priceless life lesson, and shown you exactly where you aren't currently free in your life. This is because triggers are actually blessings in disguise, if you decide to let them be.

Adopt a 'KAIZEN' mindset which is a mindset of continuous improvement. Kaizen is a compound of two Japanese words 'kai' meaning change, and 'zen' meaning good, and together they translate as 'good change'.

WHENEVER YOU ARE FACED WITH A PROBLEM IN YOUR LIFE YOU CAN OVERCOME IT BY USING THE KAIZEN PROCESS WHICH INVOLVES ASKING YOURSELF THESE QUESTIONS IN THIS SPECIFIC ORDER:
1. **What is the root cause of the problem?**
2. **How can I address the root cause of the problem?**
3. **Are changes being carried out by me in the specific areas of my life needed?**
4. **What impact will my continuous improvement effort eventually create?**
5. **How else can I keep improving?**

Kaizen focuses on continuous improvement, so focus on small steps and incremental changes rather than seeking perfection. Use this method to learn from your past self, compete with your present self, and then set the bar for your future self.

BELOW ARE SOME WAYS IN WHICH YOU CAN APPLY THE KAIZEN PROCEDURE IN YOUR LFIE:

1. **Set small achievable goals:** Break down larger goals into smaller, more manageable tasks. This makes it easier to measure progress and provides a sense of accomplishment, which motivates further improvement for the future.

2. **Embrace the spirit of continuous improvement:** Adopt a mindset of constantly seeking ways to improve yourself, your habits, and your skills. Look for opportunities to make small incremental changes in each area of your life.

3. **Start with self-reflection:** Regularly evaluate your current habits, routines, and behaviours, and then identify areas that can be improved, and then focus on one at a time. Be totally honest with yourself about where you currently are, also acknowledging both your strengths and weaknesses.

4. **Make small changes consistently:** Implement small changes regularly rather than trying to achieve drastic transformations overnight that never usually happen nor last for the long-term if they do happen.

5. **Seek feedback:** Ask for feedback from a few trusted friends, family members, or mentors who can provide you with constructive criticism and suggestions for improvement. Use that feedback as an opportunity to learn, grow, and then evolve into a better version of yourself.

6. **Practice mindfulness:** Cultivate mindfulness and self-awareness to observe your thoughts, emotions, and behaviours objectively, as this allows you to identify areas for improvement and then make conscious choices which are aligned with your future goals.

7. **Experiment, reflect, and repeat:** Treat your life as an ongoing experiment by trying out different things, approaches, techniques, and strategies to see what works best for you and what doesn't. Once you know, then stop doing what doesn't work and keep doing what does, and then constantly test, review, and refine your methods.

8. **Develop good habits:** Focus on building positive habits that align with your goals and life vision, remembering that consistency is key, so create systems and routines that support your desired behaviours and outcomes.

9. **Celebrate progress:** Acknowledge and celebrate your achievements no matter how small they are, because a win is a win whatever size. Recognise the effort and progress you've made as this will provide you with motivation to continue your improvement journey.

10. **Keep learning:** Never stop learning and expanding your knowledge by reading books, taking courses, attending workshops, and seeking out new opportunities for personal growth and development. The more you learn, the more you'll be able to apply new ideas and concepts to improve your life.

You need to push forwards despite any perceived failures or potential fuck-ups, because if you don't, then one day you are going to regret not taking action and it isn't going to be possible to ever go back and re-do any incomplete actions. Don't ever let the thought of making a mistake stop you from making moves forwards towards the life you desire and dream about. Take full ownership of your past decisions, actions, and mistakes, then use them as learning opportunities to grow and improve moving forwards in the future.

CHAPTER CHALLENGE
Whenever you find yourself at the centre of a S-H-I-T storm, start by seeing things for exactly how they are, but never worse than what they *actually* are. By doing this you can then get to the real truth of the situation and be more able to deal with the cards that you've been dealt. Challenge yourself to STOP looking at the 'losses' and START looking for the lessons.

ASK YOURSELF THESE TWO QUESTIONS:
1. **What is this difficult situation trying to teach me?**
2. **What can I learn from this difficult situation?**

Whenever you're feeling S-H-I-T sometimes all it takes is YOU to check in with YOU and have a mental meeting with yourself. A great starting point is to use the HALT strategy to ask yourself am I feeling:

Hungry
Angry
Lonely
Tired

And if all of these check out ok then next it's time for you to look at your surroundings, because if you are surrounded by crap then of course this will affect how you feel. Also start to evaluate what you've recently been doing on a daily basis to confirm that the actions you've been taking align with the person who you desire and dream of becoming.

If you find yourself in a situation where you feel everything is going to S-H-I-T then I challenge you to challenge yourself, to have a paradigm shift and start seeking out the positives. Because how you interpret your toughest of times will determine your actions and decisions from then on. Your thoughts will create your feelings, your feelings will determine your actions, and your actions will ultimately produce your results.

"If you change the way you look at things the things you look at change."

FORGIVENESS IS FREEDOM

Throughout this priceless journey of life, we will all get S-H-I-T thrown at us, and it can feel just like someone has just literally thrown faeces in our faces. It's nasty, it feels crap, and it usually brings out the worst of our emotions. Please understand that whatever's happened in the past has happened. It's impossible to go back and change it, but you can accept it, learn from it, and then focus on moving forwards as a better version of you. You can do this by forgiving those situations, forgiving those people, and most importantly by forgiving yourself!

With all of the S-H-I-T I had suffered in the past, many people around me were saying are you not PISSED OFF, are you not UPSET, and are you not ANGRY with all those people that once caused you pain? The honest answer was yes. Yes, I was so annoyed with those people that I once believed were the source of my suffering, but from the previous chapter we now know that suffering is a choice. By holding onto that anger from your past you are only hurting yourself. The people you're holding these negative thoughts, feelings, and emotions about have already moved on. They have forgotten about what they may or may not have done because it's old news to them, and they are focused on the future and moving forwards with their life, but you on the other hand, have stayed stuck in the past.

Just know that the only way out of these S-H-I-T situations is forgiveness. That word ANGER is such a strong word because ANGER is one letter away from the word D-ANGER and ANGER is the wind that blows out the lamp of the mind. Holding on to anger is like drinking poison and expecting the other person to die, but forgiveness is the

57

antidote. Forgive others, not because they deserve forgiveness, but because you deserve peace. If you're still holding on to that past pain, then it may hold you back there forever. You need to let go and grow!

Forgiving others and yourself, can be a difficult process, but it can also bring a sense of peace and closure which will then allow you to start moving on with your life. Forgiveness doesn't mean accepting that it was ok for them to behave in the way that they did, but it's accepting that what's happened has happened and it's now ok for you to start moving on with your life. You have to forgive and let go so that the past doesn't hold you prisoner.

I personally flipped my grudges for gratitude which helped to heal my pain. In my own mind, I forgave every single person for the things that had happened, and I thanked them for the priceless life lessons that those difficult situations taught me. Although this past pain lasted for months, and even years, this relatively short period of pain was nothing compared to the future of freedom, happiness, and fulfilment I now have in front of me. That past pain presented purpose which allowed me to learn, grow, and blossom into the positive thinking person who I am today.

SOME WAYS TO START THE PROCESS OF FORGIVENESS INCLUDE:

1. **Acknowledge and accept your feelings:** It's normal to feel angry, hurt, or resentful after someone has wronged you, but you need to feel those emotions without judging yourself.

2. **Understand the other person's perspective:** Try to understand what that person had going on in their life during that moment and remember that people are often driven by their own pain and insecurities.

3. **Let go of the need for revenge:** Holding onto feelings of revenge will only prolong your present pain. Understand that the best 'revenge' is no revenge at all, but to forgive, move on, and then become the very best version of yourself and leave all the S-H-I-T behind.

4. **Practice self-compassion:** Be kind and understanding with yourself as you work through the process of forgiveness. Remind yourself that forgiving yourself and others is a journey, and that it also takes time.

5. **Consider seeking professional help:** If you find it difficult to forgive and let go, or if it's causing you deep distress, then consider seeking the help of someone who specialises in guiding others through this process.

CHAPTER CHALLENGE

Sit somewhere quiet with no distractions and take out your journal. Write a letter of forgiveness to the people who hurt you in the past, and also write a letter of forgiveness to yourself. (You don't actually have to send it to them)

IF YOU NEED SOME HELP THEN BELOW IS A WAY YOU COULD STRUCTURE YOUR LETTER TO GET STARTED:

1. **Address the person you are writing to and the situation you are forgiving them for.**
2. **Clearly express your feelings and the impact it had on your life.**
3. **Acknowledge your own role in the situation and take responsibility for your actions.**
4. **Offer forgiveness and make it clear that you forgive them.**
5. **Explain why you have chosen to forgive them.**
6. **Wish the person well for the future.**

"Forgiveness is a gift you give yourself."

FACE YOUR S-H-I-T

There is a huge difference between facing your problems and avoiding them. Facing your S-H-I-T is usually quite uncomfortable and somewhat painful, however it's avoidance that causes the real long-term pain. It's so easy to go through life sweeping S-H-I-T under the carpet, but just because you can't see it, doesn't mean it's not there, and the more you hide it under there, the harder it will be to clear up when you have no other option but to face the faeces.

If you don't fully fix the root cause of your issue, you'll be forever clearing up the mess around you. This is pretty grim, but I want you to imagine that you have a leaky toilet. You know exactly where the leak is coming from, but it requires you to take uncomfortable action to strip it down, to source the parts, and to then spend some time making the correct repair. With a little bit of research, you could most probably fix the leak yourself, but if you paid for a professional to have a look, you know for certain that they could resolve your problem a lot quicker than you could by trying yourself. Instead, you convince yourself that everything's ok because it's only dripping out slowly over a period of time and you decide not to take any action at all.

Weeks go by and there is a small build-up of moisture around the base of the toilet, so you begin to wipe it up with a cloth on a daily basis. By the end of the month, it's starting to drip so you decide to place a bucket under the leak. You start to tell yourself that it may be wise to price up the repair and get the leak sorted sooner rather than later. Before you know it, you come home one day and there is S-H-I-T everywhere, and by that, I mean there is water all over the floor which has now leaked into other areas of your home. Now, you don't only have to repair the toilet, but you now need to replace the floor tiles that have gotten water under them, and also repair all of the other damage that's been caused as a result. What started as a relatively small issue very quickly escalated into a huge problem, and now you're really regretting not taking action when you first saw those warning signs.

This is the same in your life. If you don't go to the source of your problem and fix that issue (which sometimes requires professional help) you will inevitably find yourself in a real S-H-I-T situation in the future. Ignoring those uncomfortable little drips in your life will cost you greatly in the long run, because those drips are the warning signals telling you that something isn't quite right. You get to choose whether you want to potentially get messy in the moment by fixing that leak, or to mask the mess by numbing your present problems with things like drink, drugs, food, work, and sex. Be very aware that if you don't address your current issues, then you're most likely going to see the S-H-I-T show up as pain in different parts of your life down the line. Sure, you may feel briefly better in the moment by covering up your pain, but by avoiding the bad stuff you're also avoiding the future good stuff, ultimately will take you a lot longer to find out what it is that you really want. The sooner you face it, the sooner you'll fix it. Know that life can either be hard now and easy later, or easy now and hard later and the choice is completely yours!

BELOW ARE SOME STEPS TO HELP YOU DEAL WITH THE PROBLEMS IN YOUR LIFE:

1. **Acknowledge the problem:** Denial or avoidance will not make the problem go away. Take a moment to acknowledge the issue you're facing and accept that it exists.
2. **Stay calm and composed:** Try not to let emotions overwhelm you. Take deep breaths and find your inner calm, because a clear mind will help you think more rationally and make better decisions.
3. **Break it down:** Often, problems can seem overwhelming when viewed as a whole. Break the problem down into smaller, more manageable parts. This will make it easier to address each component one step at a time.
4. **Analyse and understand the problem:** Take time to understand the root cause of the issue. Ask yourself questions like, "What led to this problem?" and "What factors are contributing to it?" Understanding the problem will help you find appropriate solutions.
5. **Seek support and advice:** Don't hesitate to reach out to friends, family members, or mentors for advice and support. Sometimes an outside perspective can offer valuable insights and potential solutions.
6. **Explore different solutions:** Brainstorm and come up with multiple solutions to address the problem, then consider the pros and cons for each approach.
7. **Choose the best course of action:** After evaluating the various solutions, choose the one that you believe is the most effective and feasible.
8. **Take action:** Implement the chosen solution, because taking action is crucial to making progress.

9. **Learn from setbacks:** It's possible that your initial attempts might not work as planned. If this happens don't be disheartened. Instead view setbacks as opportunities to learn and improve your approach.

10. **Stay persistent and patient:** A positive attitude can go a long way in helping you face challenges, so focus on the progress you make rather than dwelling on the obstacles.

11. **Practice self-care:** Make sure to take care of yourself physically and emotionally, by engaging in activities that help you relax and reduce stress.

12. **Learn from the experience:** Every problem is a chance to grow and learn. Reflect on the experience and identify what you've learned to apply it to future challenges.

13. **Seek professional help:** If the problem is particularly complex or overwhelming, then don't hesitate to reach out and seek help from a professional in that specific area of your life.

Facing potential problems and the existing issues in your life can be challenging, but with the right mindset and approach you can navigate through them much more effectively. Remember that problems aren't permanent, but facing those issues is part of becoming better and the beginning of building a great life. Nobody will go through life without encountering challenges, but what really matters is how you approach and handle them. By adopting a proactive and positive mindset, you can become more resilient and capable of whatever comes your way.

When I was going through a real S-H-I-T situation I was numbing myself mainly through drink, drugs, and work. You may question why work is a form of numbing?

Ultimately, being a work addict isn't much different to being a drug addict. This is because when I was depressed, I was constantly working all the hours under the sun so I could avoid facing my current challenges, and I would use complex car problems to try and cover up my complex life problems. However, the only difference from being a work addict to being a drug addict is that society seems to congratulate those who are constantly working their asses off and taking no time off for themselves. If you find yourself avoiding certain things in your life through any of these ways or means, then I challenge you to be consciously aware and realise that although you think you are self-soothing your current pain, you are actually going to make it much worse in the long run. Just realise that there is a huge difference between self-love and self-destruction.

Life is a movie and we as individuals are all the heroes of our own unique scripts. The main character in all action movies will always face immense struggle and pain on that journey towards their end goal, and that's what makes a movie so good. It would be pretty short and S-H-I-T if that wasn't the case. But what is it that keeps us watching these types of movies? It's so we can follow the hero's journey and root for them along the way. The funny thing is that you'll happily do it for some fictional character, but you need to also start doing the same for your life. You need to not only be your biggest fan, but to also remember that you are the star of your own show. So, if you feel like you're at that difficult middle stage of your movie in your own life, then I want you to know that you must dig deep and find the courage to push through to the next chapter. Don't give up now because, is this really how you want your story to end? Put your hand on the left side of your chest. I hope you can feel that thumping? That means you are alive, and as long as that beautiful heart of yours is still beathing then you can decide exactly how your movie ends. Whatever you do, anytime you find yourself in a crap situation, don't sit there. Get up and get moving knowing that you determine your own destiny, so don't ever give up on yourself. We as humans all have a burning desire to become our very best selves which is blazing deep within our beautiful bodies, so if you're currently going through those tough times and have found yourself stuck in a place of darkness, then use that internal flame to light the torch which will guide you up and out towards your desired destination. Know that the future is unwritten, but it's what you do today that determines it!

CHAPTER CHALLENGE

This challenge is to face something that you know you've been putting off for quite some time. For instance, this could be having that difficult conversation with a friend, an employer, a loved one, or even a family member.

1. **Take out your journal and write down exactly what it is that you've been putting off.**

2. **Identify WHY you've been putting this thing off:**
   - **Is it a fear?**
   - **Is it a lack of knowledge or understanding?**
   - **Or is it something else?**

3. **Answer these 3 questions:**
   - **What is the worst thing that could happen by doing this?**
   - **What is the best thing that could happen by doing this?**
   - **What is the consequence of not doing anything?**

4. **What one small step could you take today to begin the process?**

5. **JUST DO IT!**
   - **Take action now.**

"If you don't face it, you won't fix it."

S-H-I-T DOESN'T HAVE TO LAST FOREVER

When I was going through that deep depression, I was my own worst enemy. This is because of the language that I was using towards myself within my own mind. I would constantly repeat things like, "I am NEVER going to be happy again," and then without even realising it, I had created a conformation bias for my current beliefs. Conformation bias means that without even realising it, your brain searches for, and processes evidence to support your pre-existing beliefs. Because I believed that I would never be happy again, my brain started filtering out all the information it was fed to only focus on the things that matched my existing beliefs. I started to then believe all the S-H-I-T that I was feeding myself and would sit there having my own self-pity party, which eventually turned into a complete S-H-I-T cycle. The more BS I would feed myself, the more I believed in that crap.

I want you to know that the words, "I am," when put together are two of the most powerful words that you'll ever say, because whatever you put after those words will shape your life. Think of the words, "I am," as a giant invisible magnet. Be very cautious with whatever you say after the words "I am…" because you will create an identity for yourself and invite whatever that is into your life without even knowing. You will start to believe what you're saying and then start acting accordingly.

For instance - You say the words:

"I am – lazy" – You become lazy.
"I am – stupid" – You become stupid.
"I am – stuck" – You become stuck.

Your mind doesn't know the difference from what's real or fake, so it can either be your best friend, or your own worst enemy. The greatest of all obstacles you'll ever have to overcome in your life are the ones you have created within your own mind, but if you change your thinking, you can literally change your life. Just like the quote says, "You are what you eat," the same is true for "You are what you think and absorb." So NEVER identify yourself with a past patten and be extremely careful with the language you are using towards yourself, because YOU are ALWAYS listening. Language is a trigger for meaning, and the meaning you give to something will then create an emotion.

Having the awareness about your own thoughts and the language you are using towards yourself is super important. This is because whenever you notice the negative thoughts that come in, you are then able to interrupt the pattern and decide to replace those disempowering thoughts with much more empowering ones. Know that you can't always choose your first thought, but you can always choose your second. When you can begin to control your thoughts, you can also begin to control your life.

Start by asking yourself, "Is this just a thought or a fact?" because the majority of the S-H-I-T that is going on up in our heads is made up by us. You can consciously choose to replace a thought with another one that is going to contribute to your personal growth. It doesn't mean lying to yourself by saying something like, "I am super happy and everything in my life is going great," when you know full well that it really isn't. It's about shifting your mindset to choose better thoughts that will positively impact your journey of self-improvement. Instead, you could say something like, "I am working on myself daily to help improve my overall happiness, and the more I do, the better I feel." As long as your actions align with this statement, then you're more likely to achieve your desired results.

CHAPTER CHALLENGE

Be the observer of your thoughts this week. Look at your thoughts as 'passing clouds' in the sky. Some will be fluffy, bright, and white, and others will be heavy, dark, and black. But remember that behind every dark cloud the sun still shines. Keep in mind that you aren't the clouds, you are just the viewer of those clouds. Whatever happens, those dark clouds are always going to pass and be replaced by another one, and it's the same for your negative thoughts. Whenever a negative or disempowering thought pops up, don't identify yourself with that thought, but consciously make the choice to replace it with two more positive ones. You can also make those positive thoughts into 'affirmations' by writing them down somewhere you will see them every single day, and then read them back to yourself. 4x in the morning and 4x at night.

EXAMPLE:
First thought: "No one loves me." – **Replaced with:** "I approve of myself and am so worthy of love."
First thought: "I'm not good enough." – **Replaced with:** "I am more than enough and can still become so much more."
First thought: "I can't do it." – **Replaced with:** "I can achieve anything that I set my mind to."
First thought: "That's too good to happen to me." – **Replaced with:** "I'm worthy of achieving all my dreams and desires."

Create affirmations that resonate with you personally which are true, present tense, and empowering, then ingrain them into your brain and integrate them into your day by repeating them over and over to yourself within your own mind regularly for maximum impact.

BELOW ARE SOME OF THE BENEFITS OF CREATING AND USING AFFIRMATIONS IN YOUR DAILY LIFE:

1. **Positive mindset**: Affirmations help you develop and maintain a positive mindset by shifting your focus towards empowering and uplifting thoughts. They reinforce positive beliefs about yourself, your abilities, and your potential, leading to increased self-confidence and self-esteem.

2. **Self-improvement:** Affirmations can be used to set and achieve personal goals. By repeating positive statements related to your desired outcomes, you reinforce your commitment and motivation to work towards them. This helps you stay focused, overcome obstacles, and then develop new habits and behaviours that align with your goals.

3. **Stress reduction:** Affirmations can serve as a tool to manage stress and anxiety. When you repeat calming and reassuring statements, you create a sense of inner peace and security. They can help counter negative self-talk and replace it with soothing and encouraging thoughts, in return reducing stress levels and promoting emotional well-being.

4. **Enhanced performance:** Affirmations can improve performance in various areas of life, including learning, work, sports, or other creative activities. By repeatedly affirming your own capability, skills, and ability to succeed, you enhance your self-belief and optimize your performance, resulting in maximum achievement. This positive mindset can also lead to increased focus, motivation, and resilience in the face of future challenges.

5. **Improved self-belief and self-worth:** By regularly reinforcing positive statements about your own value, strengths, and capabilities, you cultivate a deep-rooted belief in your worthiness and potential. This creates a healthy self-image and promotes a positive relationship with yourself.

6. **Overcoming limiting beliefs:** Affirmations can challenge and overcome limiting beliefs that hold you back from reaching your full potential. By consciously replacing negative and self-defeating thoughts with positive and empowering affirmations, you reshape your mindset and create new possibilities for personal growth and success.

Understand that the power of the subconscious mind is so immense that it cannot tell the difference between what's true and what's not. So, if you're speaking S-H-I-T about yourself, your brain will believe everything you say. However, if you speak positively about yourself and your own abilities, then this will have a much more positive effect on your life.

"Whatever you repeatedly say to yourself you will believe and eventually become."

FOCUS ON THE GOOD S-H-I-T

Have you ever really struggled to find and buy something very specific for someone? Let's say that it could be a Christmas or birthday present for somebody for instance. Everywhere you look you can't seem to find it, and as you need it quick, you then end up going for the second option. However, once you've given that person their present, you start seeing the exact thing you were desperately looking for literally everywhere! The reason for this is because of something in your brain called the Reticular Activating System (RAS), which is basically your brains filtering system to help you see the things that you want to see. It takes what you're currently focusing on (what you're tuned into) and then creates a filter to support that, and it will only let in the things that you're currently searching for without you even noticing. So, it's vital to be 'tuned in' to the correct frequency of the things that you want to attract into your life.

You can't live a positive life whilst tuned in to a negative frequency. Just like a radio, you will never pick up an FM station if you're tuned in to an AM frequency. Imagine driving to the airport in your car and you're trying to tune into KISSTORY which is playing those summer bangers to get you in the mood for your weekend getaway. You know that the station you're looking for is 100.00 FM, but today you're impatient, frustrated, and starting to get angry as you are really struggling to find it. It gets to a point where you are so pissed off with it, rather than slowing down and making sure everything is as it should be, or even asking your friend in the passenger seat for some help, you just say, "I can't do it because the signal round here is S-H-I-T," and then you end up driving for another hour in silence.

Little did you know that when you almost dropped your protein shake whilst racing back from the gym yesterday evening, that you accidently knocked the radio with your hand. It wouldn't ever be possible to find an FM station as the radio was now on an AM frequency. Just like in your life, you will also attract certain things towards you depending on the frequency that you are currently vibrating at. You can't be putting out negativity and expect to live a positive life, because the more you focus on all the perceived negative things in your life, the more you are going to attract those negative things towards you.

I mentioned the words 'tuned in' because (believe it or not) every single thing on this earth is moving. It's vibrating. Our bodies are made up of a collection of approximately 30 - 50 trillion cells that are all continuously vibrating. Of course, when you look at yourself in the mirror you see yourself as a physical structure, but in reality, you are a group of microscopic cells that are constantly vibrating. Even though you are a physical object, just like this book in your hand, if you zoomed in, and in, and in, you would see all the cells vibrating and moving. The only difference between you (solid/physical) and something not physical (GAS) is that you are vibrating at a lower frequency. Bearing that in mind, every single person is vibrating at a certain frequency. In life you don't get what you want, you get what you are. If you're a person who is always negative, you are 'tuned in' to a 'negative frequency' and you will attract those negative things into your life. This goes back to the law of attraction which we mentioned in previous chapters.

Whether you're aware of it or not, whatever it is that you are 'looking for' is also looking for you. If you think your life is S-H-I-T, then it is. If you think your life is great, then it is. It's as simple as that. Because life is a mirror and we as individuals are all magnets. In simple terms, like attracts like. If you want to attract the positive things into your life, it will never work if you're still tuned into the negative frequency. You must start vibrating on a more positive frequency in order to attract the positive things into your life. It sounds easy right? Well, it is. Think of a time when you were last trying to find or solve something. How did getting angry and annoyed at that situation help you overcome your issue? Did you suddenly find that thing or solve that problem? If you're anything like me, I'm sure you're thinking, "Well it didn't help at all." You may remember that it was actually when you calmed down, took a deep breath, focused on what you did want rather than what you didn't want, that you were then able to sort things out. Know that as you think, you vibrate, and as you vibrate, you attract.

BELOW ARE SOME OF THE BENEFITS OF FOCUSING ON THE GOOD ASPECTS OF LIFE:
1. **Improved mental health:** By concentrating on the positive aspects of life, you can reduce stress, anxiety, and depression. Positive thinking can help build resilience making it easier to cope with life's challenges.
2. **Increased happiness:** Emphasizing the good in your life can lead to a greater sense of contentment and joy, and gratitude for what you have can bring a sense of fulfilment and satisfaction.
3. **Enhanced physical health:** Studies have shown that positive thinking is associated with better cardiovascular health, a stronger immune system, and lower levels of stress-related hormones.

4. **Better relationships:** A positive attitude can lead to improved interactions with others.
5. **Increased productivity and creativity:** A positive mindset can boost motivation and creativity, leading to improved problem-solving and innovative thinking.
6. **Resilience during tough times:** When you focus on the good aspects of life, you develop a reserve of positivity that can help you navigate through difficult times with greater strength.
7. **Attracting positivity:** Positive energy tends to attract positive experiences and people into your life.
8. **Better decision-making:** Positive thinking can enhance your ability to make rational and clear decisions by reducing the influence of negative emotions and biases.
9. **Enhanced self-esteem:** Emphasizing the positive aspects of yourself and your accomplishments can improve your self-esteem and confidence.
10. **Longer lifespan:** Some research suggests that individuals with a positive outlook on life may live longer and have a reduced risk of certain health conditions.

Focusing on the good parts of life can have numerous positive effects on one's well-being and overall outlook, but it's essential to understand that focusing on the good doesn't mean ignoring or denying the challenges and difficulties. Acknowledging and addressing negative aspects is also important for personal growth and problem-solving. Having a balance between acknowledging the negatives and embracing the positives can lead to a more fulfilling and optimistic life.

CHAPTER CHALLENGE

Now it's time to stop focusing on the things that you don't want, because you will end up attracting those things into your life. Energy flows where attention goes, so focus only on the things that you DO want in your life.

START CREATING THE HABIT OF FOCUSING ON:
1. All the good things that you want to bring into your life.
2. Noticing when you're vibrating on a negative frequency and then start stepping into a more positive vibration by:

   - **Being thankful for everything you have. (Gratitude)**
   - **Doing something for someone else. (Service)**
   - **Meditation. (Silence)**
   - **Eating healthy.**
   - **Exercise.**
   - **Consuming 'high-vibe' content. (Music/Books)**
   - **Walking outside in nature.**

You get more of what you focus on in life, and the great thing about that is that you get to personally choose exactly what it is that you focus on in your life, safe in the knowledge that whatever it is that you seek, you will eventually find.

Hate has 4 letters, so does Love.
Enemies has 7 letters, so does Friends.
Lying has 5 letters, so does Truth.
Negative has 8 letters, so does Positive.
Under has 5 letters, so does Above.
Cry has 3 letters, so does Joy.
Anger has 5 letters, so does Happy.
Wrong has 5 letters, so does Right.
Hurt has 4 letters, so does Heal.

This above goes to show that life is a double-edged sword and that there is an opposite to everything. If you've been blessed with the ability to open your eyes today, then you've been gifted two priceless gifts which are, another chance, and another choice. So consciously choose the better side of life and transform every negative into a positive, because that's what's going to help you feel better, and also help you become better.

"What you focus on expands."

YOUR BEST RELATIONSHIP

Going through a long-term relationship breakup was the toughest thing that I've ever gone through in my life, and at the time the pain was almost unbearable. If you're currently going through that challenging period of your life right now, then I want to tell you that everything's going to eventually work out for the better, and also I want to share some tips and tools which I personally used to help me and guide you through these difficult times. Remember that healing takes time, and everyone's journey is unique. Be patient with yourself and trust that with time, you will be able to move forward and eventually find true happiness.

I always suggest to anyone going through a relationship breakup to first pull out a pen and paper then brain dump all their thoughts onto that piece of paper. From experience I know how difficult it is to even think straight at this moment in your life as your mind is completely filled with the S-H-I-T that's taking up all the space within your skull. Don't overthink what you need to write, just let the pen do the work and get it all out.

Next, I say that you should write a letter, not only telling that person what you really thought, or how you really felt about what happened, but also to forgive them. I know this may sound difficult, and that you may feel you 'can't' forgive them for what they did, but by doing this it shows to both you and them that you have now come to terms with what happened, and that you are ready to move on with your own life. Calm down, you don't have to send this letter to them, but there are a couple of things that you could do with it.

1. **Keep it somewhere safe for only your eyes to read if you ever felt the need to.**
2. **Take it to a safe environment for you to be able to burn it, which will then symbolise the end of that relationship.**

BELOW ARE SOME MORE WAYS WHICH CAN HELP YOU GET OVER A RELATIONSHIP BREAKUP:

1. **Allow yourself to grieve:** It's normal to experience a range of emotions after a breakup, including sadness, anger, and confusion. Give yourself permission to feel these emotions and allow yourself to grieve the loss of the relationship.
2. **Cut off contact:** Consider having a period of no contact with your ex-partner, as this can create a space for healing and preventing any unnecessary emotional confusion. Start by removing their contact information from your phone, and also unfollowing them on social media.
3. **Seek support:** Reach out to friends, family, or a therapist who can provide a listening ear and emotional support. Talking about your feelings and experiences can be therapeutic and help you gain perspective.
4. **Take care of yourself:** Focus on self-care during this time. Engage in activities that bring you joy, such as exercising, pursuing hobbies, spending time in nature, or practicing mindfulness and meditation. Take care of your physical health by maintaining a balanced diet, getting enough sleep, and practicing good hygiene.
5. **Reflect on the relationship:** Use this opportunity to reflect on the relationship and what you've learned from it. Take time to understand your own

needs, desires, and personal growth. This reflection can help you avoid repeating similar patterns in future relationships.

6. **Avoid rebound relationships:** Give yourself time to heal before entering a new relationship. Jumping into a new relationship too soon may prevent you from fully processing your emotions, finding closure, and figuring out what it is that you really want.

7. **Set goals and focus on personal growth:** Use this period of transition to set new goals for yourself and focus on personal growth. Invest in your hobbies, career, education, or any other aspect of life that you want to develop and improve. This can help you regain a sense of purpose and build confidence.

8. **Practice self-compassion:** Be gentle with yourself and practice self-compassion throughout the healing process. It's normal to have setbacks or difficult moments, so treat yourself with kindness and understanding.

Lastly, I want to remind you once more of how important forgiveness is after a relationship breakup, and how you should never focus on trying to get 'revenge' on that person for what they may or may not have done. Understand that the greatest thing you can do is to focus on falling in love with yourself, and to also focus on becoming the very best version of you. You must give yourself some well-needed time alone before entering a new relationship, as you first need to get to know who you truly are in order to then be able to upgrade who you are as a person. If you are jumping from relationship to relationship because you haven't yet learned the valuable lessons from the previous one, then you'll keep attracting the same type of person towards you but in different bodies until you do.

Society seems to think that if someone is single and feeling lonely, and things start going wrong in their life, then they should, "find themselves a partner," and then miraculously all their problems will disappear. This is not true, and if you're feeling lonely it's not normally because you're alone, but because you aren't yet feeling complete yourself. Another person will not solve your loneliness, and this is why many relationships fail. It's because people go into relationships thinking someone else is going to fill the emptiness they currently feel inside themselves. If you get into a relationship purely to solve your loneliness then the sad fact is that you probably haven't solved what's 'missing' in your life, but you have involved someone else in your own internal issue. With this being said, don't ever look for external solutions for your own personal problems.

Before you begin building a relationship with anyone else you need to make sure that you have already built the most important relationship that you'll ever be in, and that is the relationship with yourself. So many are searching for relationships when the one they have with themselves is S-H-I-T. You must first create the best relationship with yourself because you have to be with yourself for the rest of your life, and the relationship with oneself will last forever, whether you currently like it or not.

Self-love is so important because if you don't even love yourself, then how do you expect that anybody else is going to love you? A real relationship involves two beautiful humans that are already whole and complete who come together, and once they do, their energies combined start to complement and elevate each other at the same time. So many people are jumping from relationship to relationship looking for that 'perfect person', but the truth is that you're never going to find them as you are coming from a place of desperation. So, stop begging to find the perfect partner, and start becoming the perfect partner. Be the person who you would want to attract, and by doing that you will start actually attracting your own 'perfect' person. You need to pull out your journal, write everything you would like in a 'perfect' partner, and then become it yourself. Because if you don't already have all the traits and habits of that perfect partner, then what's making you think you're going to attract someone like that towards you?

I had grown up with the belief that as you grow older and find yourself in a relationship, that you always had to put your partner first and do everything you possibly can to make them 'happy'. However, I later found out that this backwards belief was a complete load of S-H-I-T because in life you cannot 'make' someone happy, and you shouldn't even try to! True happiness doesn't come from anyone or anywhere but from within your own head. This is because true happiness isn't a temporary feeling that comes and goes, but it is an internal state of mind. You can choose how you feel in any given moment, so with that being said, please understand that happiness is a choice. You should never rely on somebody else for happiness or to sort your issues out, because in a real relationship one person is not better than the other, and neither one will make the other truly happy with themselves.

I spent years doing everything I thought I could to make my partner happy. Of course, sometimes it seemed to have worked, and other times not so much. I remember I went through a stage of buying her small gifts on a frequent basis believing I was going to make her happy, and that by doing so she would love me even more. Another hard truth is that you can't make someone love you by means of purchasing presents for them, so don't ever think you're going to force someone to love you more by giving them gifts, because you can never buy true love or purchase a real relationship. Realise that when you are trying to force love, the other person will pick up on your energy and they will start losing respect for you.

I had become reliant on my partner believing that she provided me with happiness, and I convinced myself that anytime I wasn't with her, I wasn't happy. Now looking back, the truth is that she didn't give me happiness, and neither would anybody else. This is because I wasn't happy with myself, and it was only until I had nobody but myself could I then begin to start strengthening my relationship with me. In that relationship I had completely lost my true self because I had my whole identity wrapped up in that relationship, and when that relationship ended, I almost did too. I didn't know who the fuck I was anymore and didn't have a clue about what to do with myself. I didn't know what I liked, and I didn't know what I wanted as I was so focused on what 'we' liked and wanted. In a relationship you have to work together and make agreements together, but on the other hand it's necessary to know exactly who you are as an individual, and to also understand your own unique dreams and desires.

It's so important to have your own hobbies and interests and then take time away from your partner to explore and enjoy them, because this gives you periods where you are separated to then enjoy your own time. Also, when you are away from your partner you start to think how much you miss them, and you remember to appreciate the time you do have with them that much more. In a relationship you don't need to agree on everything that the other person agrees with or believes in, plus you must have your own thoughts and beliefs. I admit that for a long period I would not speak my truth as I didn't want to upset my partner, and I would say the things that I thought she would agree with or want to hear.

Towards the end of that relationship, I had completely lost myself because I didn't have a fucking clue who Ryan Nurse was anymore. I had come down with a severe case of the disease, 'permanently trying to please'. I was constantly trying to impress my partner, I was constantly trying to prove my worth, and I was constantly saying sorry for things that I didn't even know I had supposedly done wrong. In a real relationship you don't ever need to prove your worth because your partner should already know it, hence why they are with you, and the same goes for you about them. They say that 'love is blind' and it bloody is. I've done it and I'm sure many of you have also done it too; it's easy to change who we truly are and go against our own values in order to try and impress someone else. Whatever you do, don't lose yourself in a relationship, because no relationship is worth your own soul, sanity, or self-worth. You should never need to question if you're 'good enough' for that person because you should know your own value. Always be your true self, and if the other person doesn't like who you truly are, then I'm sorry to say that maybe they aren't the right one for you. A person who truly loves you for being you, may not like everything you do, say, or believe in, however they will accept who you are as a whole, flaws and all.

If you're in a relationship and feel like you can't be your true self, then you really need to consider if it's worth pursuing, or if it's time to call it a day, because if things aren't quite right now, then do you really think that they are going to get better with time? When someone disrespects you in a relationship, then you really need to think about leaving, because as soon as there is no respect, there is no relationship. If your intuition is telling you to get out, then you best listen to it because I've personally never known a time when my gut feeling about someone, or something wasn't correct. This is because your gut already knows what your brain hasn't yet figured out. Many think that the worst thing in life is to end up all alone, so they choose to stay put in vile relationships that aren't serving or supporting their overall health or happiness, but the truth is that the worse thing is to end up with people who make you *feel* all alone. So, whatever you do, don't let your thoughts of loneliness drive you back to a toxic relationship, and realise that the most toxic thing you can do is to ignore the bad in someone just because you 'love them'.

BELOW ARE SOME WAYS IN WHICH YOU CAN BEGIN TO BUILD A SOLID ROMANTIC RELATIOINSHIP:
1. **Self-reflection and self-awareness:** Take time to reflect on who you are and to also understand your own values, goals, and aspirations. Then take time to recognise your strengths, weaknesses, and areas for personal growth. Having self-awareness allows you to enter a relationship with a clear understanding of yourself, which in turn helps you make better choices, and also to communicate more effectively with the other person.

2. **Self-love and self-care:** Prioritise self-love and self-care in your life by treating yourself with kindness, compassion, and respect. Also engage in activities that add to your overall joy, happiness, and well-being. It is vital to do more of the things that nurture your physical, emotional, and mental well-being because when you love and care for yourself, you then become more capable of offering love and care to others.

3. **Set healthy boundaries:** Establishing and maintaining healthy boundaries is crucial for any type of relationship. This is because when you respect your own boundaries it demonstrates self-respect, and then sets the stage for a great relationship to be built on mutual respect and understanding.

4. **Develop independence:** Foster a sense of independence and individuality by pursuing your own interests, hobbies, and life goals. It's also super important to maintain your own friendships, relationships, and support systems with other people.

5. **Work on yourself:** Engauge in personal growth and self-development by continuously striving to become the very best version of yourself. This could be by means of exercising, reading certain self-help books, attending therapy or counselling sessions, joining certain clubs or groups, visiting seminars, practicing self-reflection, and even meditation. By investing in yourself and your own personal growth, you bring more to the table in a relationship which in return contributes to its long-term success.

6. **Effective communication skills:** Work on developing strong communication skills by expressing your personal thoughts, feelings, and needs, but also practice active listening when your partner is doing the same. Effective communication from both people in a relationship promotes understanding, trust, and encourages constructive discussions.

7. **Emotional intelligence:** It's important to understand and manage your own emotions, but to also be sensitive to the emotions of others in any relationship. This is because emotional intelligence creates a deeper connection, which will then help resolve any negative challenges within a relationship. Recognizing and regulating your own emotions, and also expressing empathy to the other person, helps create a feeling of emotional intimacy which shows the other person how much you care about them and your relationship together.

Being a well-rounded independent individual enhances your overall attractiveness and ensures that you will enter a romantic relationship as a complete person, rather than solely relying on your partner for happiness or fulfilment. If you are already in a relationship, just know that an emotionally healthy relationship involves two individuals who are already whole and complete and who come together and enhance each other's lives by supporting, respecting, and valuing the other person. There is no 'other half' or 'better half' to a relationship because you both already know exactly who you are and what you want in life. You both prioritise your own needs, emotions, and values and aren't co-dependent on the other person.

BELOW ARE SOME SIGNS THAT INDICATE YOU ARE IN AN EMOTIONALLY HEALTHY RELATIONSHIP:

1. **Open and effective communication:** You and your partner can express your feelings, thoughts, and concerns openly and honestly. You feel comfortable discussing both positive and negative aspects of your relationship without fear of judgement or facing future consequences. You don't have to constantly worry what your partner is going to think or worry if they are going to be mad, upset, jealous, or mean.

2. **Trust and honesty:** There is a solid foundation of trust between you and your partner, where you both feel completely secure in the knowledge; you can rely on each other, and honesty is a priority in your relationship, and secrets and lies are non-existent.

3. **Mutual respect:** You and your partner treat each other with complete respect, considering each other's feelings, opinions, and boundaries. You value each other's independence, and both support each other's goals, aspirations, dreams, and desires. Neither of you discredit, invalidate, or minimize the other persons emotions or concerns, and neither of you would say something like, "stop worrying so much," or "stop being insecure."

4. **Emotional support:** Both partners provide support to each other during their most challenging times, in return, each individual feels comfortable fully expressing vulnerability and seeking comfort or advice from the other. Your partner should help make your trauma and anxieties better and not worse.

5. **Healthy conflict resolution:** Disagreements and conflicts are normal in any relationship, however, in an emotionally healthy relationship, you and your partner should be able to communicate calmly, listen actively, and work together to then resolve any issues and find resolutions that satisfy both individuals. Both of you can admit when you're in the wrong, are able to let go of issues relatively quickly, don't hold grudges or keep score, and are always trying to improve the relationship.

6. **Independence and interdependence:** You and your partner maintain a healthy balance between independence and togetherness. You both respect each other's need for personal space, hobbies, and friendships, while also enjoying shared activities and quality time together. While you might be happy together, you're each also able to be happy when you are apart.

7. **Equality and fairness:** Your relationship is built on a foundation of equality, where decisions are made together using a sense of fairness to share responsibilities, chores, and even larger decisions that need to be made.

8. **Supportive of individual growth:** Both partners encourage personal growth and development for each other, they both support one and other's dreams and goals, and they also celebrate the success achieved by that individual.

9. **Emotional and physical safety:** You feel emotionally and physically safe in your relationship as there is no physical or mental abuse, and you feel completely comfortable to express your true self without fear of harm or harsh criticism.

10. **Shared values and goals:** You and your partner have compatible values, goals, and visions for the future, and although it isn't necessary to believe in or enjoy everything that your partner does, you both work together as a team to support each other's aspirations to then build a shared life that aligns with each of your individual desires.

Just remember that no relationship is perfect, and occasional disagreements or challenges are totally normal. However, an emotionally healthy relationship is distinguished by a strong foundation of respect, trust, open communication, and mutual support. Don't ever be someone's secret in a relationship where they don't tell others about you, and don't ever choose someone who needs to think twice about choosing you. Because in a romantic relationship a 'mixed' signal is actually a completely clear message telling you that the other person is unsure about their decision, and this is one of those red flags warning you to take a step back and reconsider your priorities. Don't ever let someone else try and change who you are to become what they need. The more time you waste trying to be what others want you to be, the more you will lose yourself. The moment you become comfortable in your own skin and enjoy spending time alone is the moment you become unstoppable. This is because when you love spending time by yourself, you will never feel the need to rely on anyone else ever again.

CHAPTER CHALLENGE

Building a solid romantic relationship with someone else which you hope will last a long time always starts with self. This means firstly starting with building the solid foundations for yourself which will end up lasting a lifetime.

BELOW ARE SOME QUESTIONS THAT I CHALLENGE YOU TO HONESTLY ANSWER:

- **Would I want to be in a relationship with me right now - If so, what are the reasons why, and if not, what are the reasons why not?**

- **What areas of the relationship with myself need attention?**

- **What things do I need to stop doing, and what things do I need to start doing to become my own perfect partner?**

- **Can I speak my truth and be myself around my partner or around a potential partner?**

BONUS CHALLENGE

This challenge requires you to take you out on a date-night with yourself. For example, you could take yourself out for a fancy dinner, to the movies, or even to participate in one of your favourite hobbies alone. Show up as the person who you would want to be in a relationship with. Treat yourself well, dress in your best outfit, and show up as if you were going on a date with your perfect partner.

Remember that building a strong romantic relationship is an ongoing process that requires patience, effort, and understanding. By starting with yourself and focusing on your own personal growth, self-love, and healthy boundaries, you are laying a super solid foundation for a long lasting and fulfilling romantic relationship. This is because the relationship you have with yourself sets the tone for all other relationships in your life.

"Don't be someone's second choice when they're your first."

UNLEARN THE S-H-I-T

A big part of life is about learning new things in order to progress. However, an even bigger part of life is about unlearning all the S-H-I-T that we've been taught throughout our childhood. From the ages of approximately 0 – 7 years old, we as humans are little living, breathing, seeing, and believing sponges; mini walking, talking, observing, and absorbing miracles. Meaning you were shaped and moulded into the person who you currently are today during that early age.

When we were born, we were all fitted with an invisible 'belief headset'. You cannot see or feel this headset, but it is 100% there, and no single headset is the same. They are all unique, and all have their own different beliefs pre-programmed into them. Throughout your childhood there will be hundreds upon thousands of beliefs now distorting and determining what you see. These beliefs were uploaded by people like your parents, family members, friends, and teachers, plus all the media that you were exposed to whilst growing up. You have viewed your whole life looking through these lenses that you've been programmed to believe to be true.

BELOW ARE THE THREE CORE BELIEFS WHICH YOU HAVE DEVELOPED WHILST GROWING UP:
1. **Your core beliefs about yourself:** These are the ones you were taught and believe about yourself which determined things like whether you were kind, smart or shy. These beliefs influenced your every thought, decision, and action depending on the things you were told and absorbed.

For example: If you were told that, "You are stupid," then you may have grown up believing that you are not good enough. Or on the other hand, if you were told that, "You can do anything that you put your mind to," then you may have then grown up believing that anything is possible with enough applied effort.

2. **Your core beliefs about others:** These taught you a lot about people which then determined your interactions with the others around you.

For example: If you experienced a loving relationship throughout your childhood, you may have learned that it's safe and ok to put your trust in others, and that helping them is a nice thing to do. However, if you experienced a painful childhood, you may have learned that people only care about themselves and everyone's out to make your life worse.

3. **Your core beliefs about the world:** These are the beliefs of everything that goes on around the world.

For example: If you experienced a caring and peaceful environment growing up as a kid, you're most likely to believe that the world is a pretty safe place. But on the other hand, your parents could have told you that the world is such a dangerous place, and to travel abroad on your own will most likely result in very bad consequences.

Everything you know up to now comes from your unique view of life and is most probably wrong. I know it sounds crazy, but please don't worry because you're not the only one. It's the same for all of us, because this reality that we see is purely personal, which makes us as adults all beautiful messes. To try and simplify this I want you think of a police witness report. Just imagine you and two friends witness somebody shoplifting and were asked to be witnesses. You were all interviewed separately, and the police officers take down all the details of that incident from your own unique personal points of view. They asked you to fill out a description form for the offender.

Your's looks like:
Sex: Male - Height: 6ft 5in - **Age:** Mid 40's – **Hair:** Bald – **Hat:** No – **Jacket:** Blue – **Trousers:** Grey jeans

Your female friends report looks like:
Sex: Male – **Height:** 5ft 5in – **Age:** Late teens – **Hair:** Short Blonde – **Hat:** No – **Jacket:** Blue – **Trousers:** Grey joggers

Your male friends report looks like:
Sex: Female – **Height:** 5ft 9in – **Age:** Early 30's – **Hair:** Long blonde – **Hat:** Yes – **Jacket:** Grey hoodie – **Trousers:** Grey joggers

As you can clearly see that these witness reports do not match up entirely. This is because we are all seeing life through our own unique view, and we are all interpreting our own reality through our own unique perception. Clearly what you see may be completely different to what someone else may see, and that's fine, because we have all had completely different upbringings, therefore we will all have entirely different beliefs. It doesn't mean that I'm right and you're wrong, it just means that we saw the event through our own limited lens. With this being said, we should always question our beliefs as they might not always be completely true.

Think back to the previous chapter when we talked about the Reticular Activating System (RAS) which is our brain's filtering system. When you believe in something, you will look for all the evidence to support and confirm your current belief, and with each piece of proof you find, that belief then becomes stronger. These limiting beliefs will affect your behaviour; if you believe you aren't smart enough to achieve something for instance, then you most likely won't put in the required effort to ever accomplish that thing in the future. It's your beliefs that will eventually determine your results. These limiting beliefs come from the childhood programming which has been downloaded into our mind over years and years. The good thing to know is that these programs can be changed, but it isn't an overnight thing. This is something what will take daily practice over a long period of time to start seeing any real results.

Millions of minors to this present day are still having outdated programs uploaded into their precious uncontaminated minds with many previous presumptions, procedures, and principals being pushed into their innocent belief systems which they are trusting to be the truth with absolutely no questions asked. Its only until one sees a better alternative to their current viewpoint of the world, which is potentially more beneficial to their life, that they can begin to question and then eventually un-learn what they already know and believe. Once they have this awareness, they can go on and relearn, then eventually replace that pre-programmed system which they had no choice but to accept, with a new and improved one which is in-line with their own unique values.

BELOW YOU CAN SEE THE DIFFERENCE BETWEEN VALUES AND BELIEFS:

While values and beliefs are related, they both serve different roles in one's life. For instance, values are the key principles that are deeply ingrained, and they guide a person's behaviour, choices, and judgement. They also dictate how one would judge what's considered 'good' or 'bad' in all areas of their life, and then reflect back to them what's important, acting as a compass for their actions. Everybody has their own unique set of core values, but realise that they are heavily influenced by a combination of their family upbringing, personal experiences, cultural influences, religion, and education. An individual's values are used to provide a sense of direction and are used to help them prioritise what matters most in their life. Values are often looked at as long lasting because they are usually relatively stable over time.

Beliefs on the other hand are the specific ideas, opinions, or assumptions that individuals hold to be true based on their life experience, and various other sources of information regardless of the evidence. Beliefs can be about a wide range of topics including religious and spiritual beliefs, social issues, scientific theories, or personal convictions for instance. Beliefs influence how individuals interpret the world, make judgements, and form opinions. They can be both conscious and unconscious and may shape an individual's attitudes, perceptions, and behaviours. Beliefs can be flexible and subject to change based on new information or experiences.

EXAMPLES OF BELIEFS INCLUDE:
1. **Religious beliefs:** Beliefs about the existence and nature of a higher power, the purpose of life, and moral guidelines based on religious teachings.
2. **Political beliefs:** Beliefs about the role of government, social issues, economic systems, and individual rights, often shaping political ideologies like liberalism, conservatism, or socialism.
3. **Scientific beliefs:** Beliefs based on scientific theories and evidence, such as beliefs in evolution, climate change, or the effectiveness of certain medical treatments.
4. **Cultural beliefs:** Beliefs influenced by one's cultural background, traditions, and customs which can also include beliefs about gender roles, family structures, or the importance of community.
5. **Moral and ethical beliefs:** Beliefs about what is right and wrong, ethical principles, and moral standards. These beliefs shape judgements on topics like honesty, fairness, and responsibility.
6. **Social beliefs:** Beliefs about social constructs and dynamics such as beliefs about race, gender, social class, and their influence on opportunities and social structures.
7. **Personal identity beliefs:** Beliefs about one's self-identity, including beliefs about personal abilities, strengths, weaknesses, and personal traits.
8. **Health and wellness beliefs:** Beliefs about health, wellness, and practices related to maintaining physical, mental, and emotional well-being such as beliefs about exercise, diet, and alternative therapies.
9. **Environmental beliefs:** Beliefs about the importance of environmental conservation,

sustainability, and the impact of human activities on the natural world.

10. **Beliefs about success and achievement:** Beliefs about what it takes to be successful, the nature of achievement, and the factors that contribute to personal or professional success.

EXAMPLES OF VALUES INCLUDE:

1. **Honesty:** Valuing truthfulness, sincerity, and ethical behaviour in personal and professional relationships.
2. **Compassion:** Valuing empathy, kindness, and concern for the well-being of others, and taking actions to help them alleviate their suffering.
3. **Integrity:** Valuing moral and ethical principles, being consistent in actions and values, and sticking to a sense of honesty and strong moral character.
4. **Respect:** Valuing the worth and dignity of all individuals, treating others with consideration, listening to varied viewpoints, and appreciating differences.
5. **Responsibility:** Valuing accountability, reliability, and taking ownership of one's actions, commitments, and obligations.
6. **Equality:** Valuing fairness, justice, and equal opportunities for all individuals, regardless of their background, gender, race, or other characteristics.
7. **Freedom:** Valuing individual rights, independence, and the right to make choices without undue interference or oppression.
8. **Environmental stewardship:** Valuing the preservation and sustainable use of natural resources and taking responsibility for protecting the environment for future generations.

9. **Family:** Valuing strong family bonds, nurturing relationships, and prioritizing the well-being and support of family members.
10. **Education:** Valuing lifelong learning, personal growth, and the pursuit of knowledge and intellectual development.
11. **Collaboration:** Valuing teamwork, cooperation, and working towards common goals in a harmonious and inclusive manner.
12. **Excellence:** Valuing high standards of performance, continuous improvement, and striving for personal or professional mastery.

In summary, values are the primary principles that guide a person's actions, while beliefs are the specific ideas one would have based on their own life experiences and the information that they have been exposed to throughout their life. Values provide a much broader framework for decision-making, whereas beliefs can be much more specific and related to certain areas of one's life. Overall, both beliefs and values play a significant part in shaping an individual's worldview, identity, and behaviours as they both contribute to influencing one's thoughts, actions, and attitudes.

Realise that just because something has been the way it's always been, doesn't meant it'll be the way it'll always be. For instance, what may have been good for your parents 20/30/40 years ago may not be so good for you now. Even if they are still trying to tell you it is, just know that you don't have to listen to or believe in what they are saying. This is because the world is constantly changing at a rapid rate, so you need to keep up to date with what's going on, and to do your own investigations, or if not, you'll be left behind believing the same old S-H-I-T as every other person stuck in their stiff minded ways. You need to question what you already know and find the facts to either prove it to be right or wrong, and don't just take what someone's told you to be gospel. You have to be willing to explore the alternatives to what you already believe to be true and be open to change. Know that the mind is like a parachute; it doesn't work if it isn't open. If you go through your life with a closed mind, then you'll likely find yourself coming face to face with a lot of closed doors.

STEPS YOU CAN TAKE TO START REPROGRAMMING YOUR CHILDHOOD BELIEF SYSTEM:

1. **Recognise that you have been programmed:** The first step in reprogramming your mind is to recognise that your thoughts, beliefs, and behaviours have been shaped by your past experiences and the people around you.
2. **Identify limiting beliefs:** Take some time to reflect on the beliefs that are holding you back. These might include beliefs about yourself, others, or the world that are not serving you.
3. **Challenge limiting beliefs:** Once you have identified your limiting beliefs, challenge them by asking yourself whether they are true and if there is evidence to support them.
4. **Replace limiting beliefs with empowering beliefs:** Replace any limiting beliefs with ones that align with your personal goals and values.
5. **Repetition of new beliefs:** Repeat your new beliefs to yourself regularly and visualise yourself living them.

6. **Surround yourself with supportive people**: Put yourself in places with people who support and encourage your new beliefs.
7. **Take action:** Take action towards your goals and put your new beliefs into practice.

Remember what we talked about previously regarding awareness. This is super important when it comes to childhood programming, because how the fuck are you ever going to escape the matrix if you're not aware that the matrix even exists. Don't forget that reprogramming your mind is a continuous process that requires patience, repetition, and commitment, so it's crucial to remember that some limiting beliefs can be deeply ingrained and may take much longer to witness and replace. So don't rush the process and don't be discouraged if you don't see immediate results.

You have to take control of your life by owning your S-H-I-T. It may not be your fault you are the way that you are, but it's your responsibility to decide who it is that you're going to become. The results you have already achieved up until now are a direct consequence of the decisions and the actions you have either taken or not taken throughout your life. Realise that it's you and you alone who is responsible for the life you have created for yourself. So, if it isn't looking like the life that you want then you must change something; doing the same things over and over will always produce the same results. Stop blaming outside forces to avoid taking accountability and start acknowledging that you have the ability and responsibility to shape your own life. Then start making choices that align with your own values and goals. Recognise that blaming external forces or other people for your circumstances will only hold you back.

<u>CHAPTER CHALLENGE</u>
Pull out your journal and start questioning the existing beliefs you aren't completely sure to be true and ask yourself if those existing beliefs are supporting and contributing towards the life you want to create for yourself.

BELOW ARE SOME WAYS OF DISCOVERING YOUR FAULTY PROGRAMMING:
1. **Identify your limiting belief/s:** Write down your limiting belief/s and then ask yourself these questions - "Is this a fact or an opinion?" – Then look for any evidence both for and against the belief. And also, these questions - "Where did I learn this from and is it contributing towards creating the life I want?" – If it's not adding to your personal growth then replace or remove it.
2. **Talk to a trusted friend or therapist:** Ask them for their honest feedback about your belief/s as they may be able to provide a different perspective or challenge your current belief in a constructive way.
3. **Imagine yourself living without the limiting belief:** Consider how your life would be different and what opportunities may arise if you were able to let go of or replace that belief.
4. **Practice mindfulness and self-compassion:** Learn to observe your thoughts without judgement and be kind and understanding towards yourself.
5. **Challenge the limiting belief:** Start talking small steps towards the opposite belief and see how it feels.

6. **Replace the limiting belief**: Consciously decide to replace your current belief with a more empowering one.

BONUS CHALLENGE

Write down all of those limiting beliefs that you currently have which aren't contributing to your overall personal growth and development on a separate piece of paper. Once you've done that, then in a safe environment take that piece of paper with all those disempowering beliefs on and burn it. This is symbolising that you won't let those fuckers rule your life or stop you from achieving greatness!

"Sometimes you have to unlearn to learn."

Don't forget to join the accountability group
and support each other along the way.

S-H-I-T MINDSET, S-H-I-T LIFE

Your mind is like a factory and the ingredients you are putting into it will be used to make the final product which is YOUR FUCKING LIFE. Whatever you do, make sure you fill your mind with positivity, whether it's the people you listen to, the places you go to, or the content you expose yourself to, because you become what you consistently consume, both consciously and unconsciously.

Every single thing you do starts within your mind, so having a good mindset is essential to living a good life. This is because your mindset can affect your mental health, emotional well-being, and overall life satisfaction. Having a strong mindset can positively impact your ability to handle challenges, build positive relationships, and make better life decisions. On the other hand, having a negative mindset can result in mental health issues, missed opportunities, and also limit your ability to achieve your full potential.

WAYS IN WHICH YOU CAN START IMPROVING YOUR MINDSET:
1. **Regular exercise:** By regularly exercising you can notice many mental benefits that include reduction in stress/anxiety, improved mood/self-esteem, increased clarity, better sleep quality, and increased productivity. This is because exercising releases 'feel-good' hormones within the brain.
2. **Practice gratitude:** By practicing daily gratitude you will notice that you improve your mood, decrease your negative emotions, and are able to focus on all the positive things you have in your life.

3. **Get enough sleep:** This one is surely a no-brainer because you can't perform at your optimum if you are only half charged. That's why it's so important to get enough sleep if you're looking to your reduce stress, increase your awareness, improve your memory, and enhance your overall quality of life.
4. **Meditation:** This is a fantastic way of slowing your mind down, processing your thoughts, focusing on what you want, and then gaining clarity on what you need to do moving forwards.
5. **Get out in nature:** Go for a walk, breath in some fresh air, and clear your mind by taking in all of what's around you.
6. **Learn new things:** Learning something new is a great way of improving your mindset, because in life it's progress that equals happiness.
7. **Read books:** Frequently reading can help improve your mindset in many ways, including, increasing your knowledge/understanding, expanding your personal perspective, improving your language skills, enhancing your focus and concentration, promoting relaxation, stimulating creativity within your mind, and contributing to your overall personal growth.
8. **Journal:** Journaling is by far one of the top ways to help improve your mindset. This is because it allows you to get everything out of your head and on to paper so that you can physically see your thoughts. This allows you to then start working out ways to untangle the mess which was washing around within your mind.
9. **Consume more positivity:** Whatever you absorb you will eventually become. So, make the conscious

decision to start filling your body, mind, and soul with more of the good stuff.

10. **Do absolutely nothing:** I use to hate being 'bored' but sometimes it can actually be a great thing to do absolutely nothing at all, give your brain a rest, and to try and completely clear your mind. Use this time to rest, relax, recharge, reset, rejuvenate, and then resume.

11. **Seek therapy or counselling:** If you feel like you've tried all of these and you're not noticing any improved changes, then realise that it's ok to reach out for professional help. Having somebody who specialises in this can help guide you through the process and give you alternative views/suggestions as opposed to what you've already tried.

Know that your mind is just like a garden, and you are the gardener. Removing negativity from your life is just like removing the weeds from your garden. If left unmaintained then without even realising, one day you're going to take a look at what you've got and suddenly see that those weeds have now taken over your entire garden. Just like you can either control your mind, or you can let your mind control you, you must take care of your mental garden every single day, because if you don't, then the S-H-I-T is going to completely take over your priceless plot. You also have to prioritise your precious patch first and water your plants before even thinking about watering anybody else's. And you have to plant the correct seeds depending on what it is that you want to grow, because you will always reap what you sow. You can't plant apple seeds and then expect an orange tree to grow, just like you can't fill your mind with negativity and then expect to live a positive life. Don't forget to pick the fruits of your labour from time to time and tase the hard work, discipline, and delayed gratification you invested into yourself and your future produce. Lastly, always look out for naughty negative neighbours who are throwing rotten seeds in your soil hoping to spoil your success. You must monitor your soil on a daily basis, just like you must monitor what it is that you are allowing access into your mind, because your soil is the foundation for a fruitful harvest, just the same as your mindset and your thoughts are the grounds for a great life. Any S-H-I-T that does get thrown your way, you must use as fertilizer to flourish, evolve, blossom, and bloom into the best version of yourself. Understand that whatever you plant into your subconscious mind and nourish with repetition and emotion, will one day become reality.

SIGMUND FREUD'S THEORY OF THE 'THREE LEVELS OF MIND' BREAKS ONE'S MIND UP INTO THREE DISTINCTIVE LEVELS, EACH WITH THEIR OWN ROLES AND FUNCTIONS WHICH INCLUDE:

1. **The conscious mind:** The conscious mind refers to the mental process and information that we are currently aware of, including our thoughts, perceptions, sensations, and feelings which we are experiencing in the present moment. For example, when you are reading this text and thinking about it, your conscious mind is engaged.

2. **The preconscious mind:** The preconscious mind contains thoughts, memories, and pieces of information that are not currently in our conscious awareness, however, can be easily accessed with some sort of effort or motivations. Just imagine the preconscious mind as a huge filing cabinet for all the past information to be stored away, but ready to access at any given moment if and when needed.

For example, if I asked you to recall a specific event from your childhood, you can bring it into consciousness from the preconscious mind.

3. **The unconscious mind:** The unconscious mind refers to a much deeper level of awareness that contains thoughts, desires, memories, and emotions that are not readily accessible to conscious awareness. These unconscious processes are believed to influence our thoughts, feelings, and behaviours even though we are not consciously aware of them. According to Sigmund Freud himself, the unconscious mind stores repressed or forgotten memories, traumatic experiences, and unresolved conflicts that can affect our behaviour and mental health.

CHAPTER CHALLENGE

This week your challenge is to really focus on yourself and work on improving your mindset. If you really want to upgrade your life, then you must first upgrade your mindset. This is because you will never solve a problem using the same version of mindset which created it in the first place. Once the week has ended and all the tasks hopefully complete, go back to your journal and do another self-assessment to see how you've scored compared to the week before.

OVER THE NEXT 7 DAYS YOU HAVE 7 DAILY CHALLENGES TO COMPLETE WHICH ARE:

1. **Workout/go walking:** Each day spend 1 full hour working out or walking without any distractions. Be completely present and focus on what you're doing.
2. **No phone:** Spend 2 hours per day where you don't look at your phone at all. By this I mean don't even pick it up to check the time.
3. **Read a book:** Each day find the time to read 3 pages of a book.
4. **Practice daily gratitude:** Each day write down 4 things you are grateful for. For instance, you could write down 2 in the morning and 2 at night. Or 4 in the morning, or 4 at night. It's entirely up to you. If you don't think this is important then just imagine you woke up tomorrow with only the things that you were grateful for today.
5. **Meditation:** Spend 5 minutes meditating per day. If you've never done this don't worry, when I say meditate it's not like you need to go and sit naked in the woods with your legs crossed whilst going "hmmmm." Well, unless you want to that is! Meditation can be done in various different ways.

For example, it can be done whilst sat somewhere in silence, whilst out walking, or whilst laying in the bath among many more. Set yourself a 5-minute timer, focus on your breath, and try to clear your mind. If your mind starts to wander it's ok, just gently redirect your focus back to your breath. If you're really struggling to stop your mind from running away, then focus on your five senses (sound, smell, sight, taste, and touch).

6. **Journaling:** Spend 6 minutes per day journaling. Again, sit somewhere nice and quiet with absolutely no distractions and get all your current thoughts out on paper.

7. **Sleep:** Make sure you get 7 hours uninterrupted sleep per night over these 7 days. Consider setting yourself a sleep routine where you limit/avoid gadgets and bright lights, starting one hour before you plan to start sleeping. You could tick two tasks off your list by trading scrolling your phone for reading or writing before calling it a night.

Know that every next level of your life will demand a different version of you.

"You will never achieve Maserati dreams with a Mazda mindset."

THOUGHTS REALLY DO BECOME THINGS

By now I'm hoping that you realise the unlimited power of your own mind, because you've seen how things like your perception can shape your reality, and you've seen how you can attract the things (both good and bad) into your life just by focusing on them. Now I want to open your mind up to something even more incredible, which is the power of your imagination!

You may be thinking this is still a bit 'woo-woo' and believe that there is no way that you could 'think' your dream life into existence, but the truth is that you absolutely can. If you still don't believe it, then I'd like to share with you a real-life example of how powerful your mind is.

I'm sure you've heard of the 'placebo effect' and if you haven't then let me explain. The placebo effect is when a 'fake treatment' like a sugar pill is prescribed to a patient. Without them even realising, they are given this 'fake drug' and it miraculously makes them feel better just because they now believe this 'miracle tablet' will help them become better. This happens because the power of belief and expectations can have a real impact on our bodies and how we feel. So even though the sugar pill doesn't actually contain any medicine at all, the user's own belief that it does, can astonishingly cause them to feel better. The exact same is for how somebody can also think themselves into a state of illness through a 'fake treatment' pill, just because that particular patient truly believes that the 'miracle tablet' they were prescribed by their doctor is going to have unpleasant effects on their health. Their own belief of this is so strong that they start to notice negative impacts after taking this pill, even though there are absolutely no medical components within this tablet.

Understand that every single thing that has ever been created, has been created twice. Once in the mind, and once in reality. Every book you've read, every phone you've held, and every movie you've ever watched. These things were all first formed in the mind of somebody else, and then secondly physically produced to share with the world. The great thing to know about this is that you are currently designing your life's movie within your own mind, and you are the main character. You get to decide what your life will look like as you are the director, producer, the writer, and the editor. You are the camera operator who is recording this whole experience called 'life' on a daily basis through your own unique set of eyes, and you get to choose exactly what it is that you focus on. At any given moment you can decide to make a plot twist, and as long as your beautiful heart is still beating, then you can decide how your story ends. So never give up on yourself and never let the best day of your life be in the past; being here right now confirms that it's still possible for you to flip the script on your life.

You could and should use your imagination to your advantage to help solve some of your current challenges, and to also add to your motivation and inspiration to achieve and receive the things you really want in your life. Just think back to when you were a young child running round in that playground at school. Remember all those thoughts, beliefs, dreams, and future goals you had. Whether it was to be on the cover of a magazine, to become an astronaut, a singer, or the next best football player of all time. The opportunities were endless. You truly believed you could and would become anything or anyone you wanted to be, and there were absolutely NO restrictions within your mind for why you couldn't. However, as you grew up you had society wrap its chains around your creativity so tightly that your future aspirations were being completely crushed. Remember what you previously learned in the chapter which explained the importance of unlearning all the S-H-I-T society had programmed into you as a child? This is why it's so crucial, because other people's limited thinking was unknowingly passed on to you and as a result contaminated your imagination, but worst of all destroyed your dreams. Don't worry, because right now you are going to start stripping back those chains to release your limitless imagination again, and to start using it to your advantage.

HERE ARE JUST SOME OF THE BENEFITS OF UNLOCKING THE POWER OF YOUR IMAGINATION:
1. **Increased motivation and inspiration:** When you can see a compelling future for yourself in the distance, you are more inclined to take greater actions to get to that place.
2. **Increased creativity and problem solving:** Using your imagination allows you to come up with a variety of 'out of the box' ideas and solutions to potentially solve more complex problems.
3. **Visualisation of future goals:** By using your imagination you can create the life of your dreams within your own mind, and then visualise what it's going to be like before you've even got there.
4. **Better decision making:** You can use your imagination to create potential scenarios within your mind, and then take actions towards achieving the preferred outcome.

5. **Reduced stress and anxiety:** Visualisation techniques can be used by creating mental images or calm and peaceful scenarios.
6. **Enhanced memory:** Using your imagination to visualise certain things makes information easier to remember, as the brain processes visual information more efficiently.

Would you believe me if I told you that the universe is only 6 inches wide? Well of course you wouldn't. But it is, so let me explain. Your unique reality exists in the space between your ears, so this means that you can decide how big or small, or how positive or negative you want your life to be. Because how reality is perceived is through the eye of the beholder. You get to choose what exists in your own reality and what doesn't, and you get to choose whether you live a life of lack or a life of prosperity and abundance. So, choose to make this infinite expanse within your mind a place of pure love, joy, happiness, and abundance.

CHAPTER CHALLENGE

This exercise requires both thinking and writing to make the most out of it, so grab your journal then go and sit somewhere relaxing with absolutely no distractions at all. If you want to you can put on some calming sounds to help quieten your mind. My personal favourite is to put on my headphones and play creativity binaural beats. This is because certain types of frequencies affect your brainwaves in different ways, and this helps me think clearer. Start to make that mental movie of what your 'perfect' day would look like within your mind, but really focus on who it is that you've become as an individual. Take a mental note of your new and improved way of living, like your daily habits and the ways you now think and feel.

YOU ARE NOW GOING TO DESIGN YOUR 'PERFECT LIFE' WITH THE HELP OF YOUR IMAGINATION:

1. **Imagine what is possible:** Begin by letting your mind run freely and start thinking as if you were a young child again. What are some of the things you'd like to create and have in your life? Start seeing the future you desire within your own mind.

2. **How does it feel:** Just imagine as if you were already there and start to focus on and feel all the emotions which you would feel if this was real.

3. **What do you look like:** Now that you're already living your dream within your mind, take note of what you look like as the very best version of yourself. How is your posture, what is the expression on your face, what clothes are you wearing, and what does your overall health look like?

4. **Put pen to paper:** Write all of this down in your journal. What was possible for you, what did you want, what and who did you have around you, how did you feel, and what did you look like as a person?

5. **Create a vision board:** Decide what you want to manifest into your life. Collect the images, quotes, and symbols that represent your dreams and desires. Choose your board, whether it's cork, paper, or even digital. Organise and arrange your materials in a way that visually represents your goals and aspirations. Once complete you need to place your vision board somewhere that you will see it on a daily basis. Then all you need to do is spend time each day looking at your vision board, imagining yourself having already achieved these goals, and then feeling the emotions associated with it.

6. **Draw your future:** It's ok, please don't S-H-I-T yourself, because you don't have to be the next Banksy or Van Gogh to do this exercise! Use whatever drawing skills you currently have to divide a page and draw a picture of your 'CURRENT REALITY' and your 'DESIRED DESTINATION'. In the middle of the two will be the bridge of the things you need to do in order to get you from where you currently are to where you want to be. This was inspired by my friend Patti Dobrowolski's 'draw your future' Ted Talk, so make sure you go and check it out online to see how you can create your own, and to learn all the benefits of doing this.

"Your imagination is the preview of what's to come."

DISCOVER AND DECIDE EXACTLY WHAT YOU WANT

I spent around 13 years in my one and only day job which gave me no sense of joy, meaning, purpose, or fulfilment. Don't get me wrong, the first 3 years of my apprenticeship were absolutely fantastic as I was challenging myself on a daily basis whilst learning new things, but then it just flatlined. In life, if we're not growing, we're dying, because it's progress that equals happiness. In that moment I wasn't progressing but instead I was just producing, and at that point in my career I had become uncomfortably comfortable. I knew deep down that I didn't really want to be there, however, I had done absolutely nothing to start the process to make the transition in the future. I let each day pass by and used to tell myself things like, "It's ok because it pays the wage," even though my soul was screaming it was time to move on. One of the main reasons I stayed stuck was because I didn't have a clue of what I wanted to achieve, or where I eventually wanted to be in the future. So, what did I do? I chose to stay put.

I worked 6 days a week and had to be at work for 8 AM each day. The crazy thing is that I used to set my alarm for 7:30. Bearing in mind I had to get out of bed, get washed and changed, eat breakfast, and then get in the car and go to work which was 10-30 minutes away depending on traffic. Because of this, most days I'd be rushing to work, I'd be frustrated, and also panicking about whether I would actually make it there on time or not, and then when I did eventually arrive, I would already be in a heightened state of stress because I was now chasing my tail. If you're not pursuing your own personal path of purpose in life, then you end up leaving everything until the very last minute, and you also put in the very minimal amount. And that was me. I'd turn up dead on time, I'd have my lunch breaks dead on time, I'd go home dead-on time, and I'd rarely go above and beyond because I didn't really want to be there. I'd regularly be saying things like, "I hate Mondays" – "I don't wanna go to work today" – "I can't wait till the end of the day" – "I can't wait till the weekend." If you find yourself constantly saying any of these things, then I believe it's your intuition trying to tell you that you're currently on the wrong path in life, and that you need to start making changes. Stop spending 5 priceless days not enjoying your life, to then use the only 2 potential days you do have trying to drown away your issues and forget them. Don't get me wrong, it's not like you should, or need, to quit your job tomorrow and just start going after something if you don't even know what it is yet, but these persistent feelings are WARNING signals to try and grab your attention to inform you that you really need to consider changing things. If you choose to ignore those signs, then you're going to stay stuck in that place of discomfort for the rest of your life until you decide to act on them. Because time will pass by and you'll let 1 year go by, which will soon turn into 10 years, and the next thing you know you'll convince yourself that you're trapped forever.

If this feels like it is hitting home for you, then I want you to know that you aren't stuck, because being stuck is a choice. If you want change, then you need to wake up and get the fuck up to start making the moves in the direction of your desired destination, rather than settling for the S-H-I-T; if you don't then you're going to really regret it one day. If something inside of you is telling you to change then don't ignore it. Don't ever get so caught up on making a living that you forget to make a life for yourself. Because the fact is that if you're in a job and you died, the following week there would be adverts put out to replace your position, however for your loved ones there would be a permanent void left in their souls which would never ever be replaced or filled.

Just realise that no matter how long you've been traveling down the 'wrong road' it's never too late to stop, check your maps, reset your sat-nav, and then turn around to start heading towards your desired destination. Understand that we will all go through either one of two different discomforts in life, which is either the temporary pain of making uncomfortable changes to become better, or the permanent pain of remaining in the exact same position and doing the exact same things. Of course, it's going to be scary, but the moment you realise the pain of staying the same exceeds the pain of change, is the exact moment your actions will overcome your anxieties. Listen to what your body is telling you because the soul does not lie, nor can it be lied to. If you want to live a life full of sadness, sorrow, and suffering then don't stop lying to your soul. If you decide to live a life of lack and a life of mediocracy then it's going to eventually drive you crazy, because if you know what you should be doing but aren't doing it then life will eat you up. You can either live your life by chance or by choice, and you get to choose whether you change or remain the same.

I've noticed that many confused young adults are diagnosing themselves with depression, when in fact they're just lacking direction, and I've also noticed they're spending their lives literally living for the fucking weekends. They go out each weekend and prioritise things like drink, drugs, pubs, and clubs, and are drowning their sorrows to try and avoid their current reality, rather than facing their S-H-I-T and coming up with a plan of action to change it. Look I'm not trying to be the 'fun police' here but realise that there is a huge difference from enjoying your youth and destroying your future. If you don't have any goal or vision in your life then that's what you'll constantly find yourself doing in different ways, shapes, or forms, because the purpose of life is to live your life on purpose, and the person without purpose will find pleasure in distractions. They will find themselves giving their priceless time away each day doing things that do not align with their true desires which, in return, makes them feel down, depressed, and directionless.

Know that a great life doesn't happen by chance but happens by choice and change. So, if you want to create a great life for yourself then you need to start living life by design and not by default. You must first make the decision of EXACTLY what you want your life to look like so that you can then start to create an action plan of how you can achieve this in the future. Understand that it's totally ok to not know your purpose right now, but it's not ok to not be in constant pursuit of it. You have to make the decision that you're going to start searching for what it is that you want, because its' ok if what you're doing in life is figuring out what you're doing in life. You have to choose to use your weekends to build the life you want, instead of trying to escape the current life you have. And it's crazy to think that your life would drastically change by repeatedly doing the same old things, because if you always do what you've always done, then you'll always get what you've always got. Don't go drinking your weekends away to then sit scrolling social media on a Sunday feeling sorry for yourself. Make the choice to start searching for what it is that you want, rather than getting to the end of your weekends with a sore head, sore thumb, and an empty wallet.

"WHAT IS MY PURPOSE IN LIFE?"

This is an extremely powerful and important question that most of us will come face-to-face at one point in or lives, and its crucial to figure out this very personal question in order to live a fully fulfilled life. When you wake up every day with intention because you are living a purposeful life, it helps drive you to places you once thought were impossible to reach, this is because purpose is a fantastic motivator.

BELOW ARE SOME OF THE BENEFITS OF KNOWING YOUR PURPOSE:
1. **Improves your self-worth and well-being.**
2. **Gives more meaning to your life experiences.**
3. **Gives you a reason to get up in the morning.**
4. **Helps you overcome obstacles in your life.**
5. **Helps you identify how you fit into the wider world.**

Ultimately, finding your purpose in life is a journey of discovery that takes time and self-reflection, but by being intentional and persistent you're more likely to discover what brings you true happiness, meaning, and fulfilment. The quicker you get started, the quicker you're likely to discover what you want in your life. Start small and realise that the path becomes much clearer the more you move forwards. So, stay open-minded, and don't put too much pressure on yourself to figure everything out in an instance. And remember that's its always ok to change your mind and try new things, because nobody has this life figured out and there is no real right or wrong track. Trust that you'll figure out if it's right or wrong for you along the way. People's purposes do change, and sometimes the path of purpose that you are currently on may be leading to an even longer path with a much greater purpose, but the most important thing is to be consciously aware whilst on your current track to check whether you're enjoying the journey or not. If you are then that's great, keep going. However, if you're not then maybe it's time for change. Just because you've been in a job or a relationship for a long period, doesn't mean that you need to stay in it, and especially if it's getting you down. Don't let your loyalty be your leash, because you are only ever just one decision away from a completely different life!

6 OF THE BIGGEST LIFE DECISION YOU'LL EVER HAVE TO MAKE:
1. **Who you're going to surround yourself with.**
2. **Where you're going to live.**
3. **Who or if you're going to marry.**
4. **What you're going to do for money.**
5. **Who you're going to be as a person.**
6. **What you're going to dedicate your life to.**

The two most important days of your life are the day you were born and the day you find out why. When you know your why for waking up each day, your pain threshold increases and you'll start to notice your ability to push through pain barriers that you once couldn't previously, and it will seem like you've gained a superhuman sort of strength that will see you through the toughest of times. You start to push yourself even harder than ever before, and you can withstand so much more of your own applied suffering. Because when you find your purpose, it gives you the strength to do things that you never thought were possible.

YOUR PURPOSE DOESN'T HAVE TO CHANGE THE WORLD!

Many think that they will never find their unique purpose as they believe that they don't have something within them that could possibly change the world, which in return stops them from even looking. Well number one, don't ever underestimate your own potential. Realise that you have greatness within you; helping just one person may not change the world, but for that one person it may change *their* world. And number two, your purpose doesn't even have to change the world. Of course, if it happens to have a greater impact and benefit a wider community then that's brilliant. You can find a sense of purpose by changing your own world, or you could find the purpose of life by contributing to change a community's world for the better. Whatever it is you do, and no matter the size of the impact, your life's purpose must matter to you the most.

People often ask the question, "What is the meaning of life?" and I believe the meaning of life is whatever meaning you want to give it. I personally think the meaning of life is to find who you truly are as a unique individual, and to share your gifts with the world. Really, the meaning of life is to find your gift, but the purpose of life is to give it away. I believe we were all put on this planet for a reason, and it isn't just by chance. Some find out the reason they are here, and sadly others don't. It's possible for you to find your purpose, and it's also possible for your purpose to find you. If you're constantly looking for why you are here then obviously, you're more likely to figure out quicker than just waiting, but once you do realise your purpose you must follow through with it whilst keeping in mind that your purpose can, and sometimes will, change along the way, and this is totally ok. There is no greater gift you could give or receive than to honour your calling, because it's why you were born and how you become fully fulfilled. Your job is what you are paid for, but your purpose is what you were made for. Your purpose is to live a life of purpose.

BELOW ARE SOME TIPS FOR ANSWERING THE QUESTION "WHAT IS MY PURPOSE IN LIFE?"

1. **Self-reflection:** Take time to reflect on your passions, interests, values, and what truly matters to you, and consider moments in your life when you felt most fulfilled and alive. Also ask yourself what activities bring you joy and a sense of purpose, and what do you find yourself doing a lot of in your free time. Think back to the time when you felt the happiest, or something you did that was the 'best time of your life!'

2. **Identify strengths and talents:** Recognise your unique strengths, talents, and skills. Consider what comes naturally to you and the things that others have praised you for in the past.

3. **Set goals and aspirations:** Think about the kind of impact you want to make in the world and the legacy you wish to leave behind. Setting meaningful goals can help you align your actions with your purpose.

4. **Explore different areas:** Be open to exploring various interests and opportunities. Sometimes your life's purpose might evolve over time, so be willing to adapt and grow.

5. **Seek inspiration:** Read books, watch documentaries, or listen to podcasts that inspire you. Learn about the journeys of other people and see how they found their own purpose.
6. **Seek support and guidance:** Engage in conversations with friends, family, or mentors who know you well and can provide valuable feedback and support. By surrounding yourself with people who already know their purpose, you are more likely to discover your own.
7. **Mindfulness and meditation:** Practicing mindfulness and meditation can help you connect with your inner self and gain clarity about what truly matters to you.
8. **Consider how you can serve others:** Quite often, finding purpose is intertwined with helping others. Reflect on how your skills and passions can be used to make a positive impact on the lives of others, and the world that we live on.
9. **What can't you accept:** There are millions of problems in this wonderful world, but is there just one of these problems which you simply can't live with? Maybe it's something that you can't just sit back and watch happen, and that there is something you want to do about it. It's something that you are willing to suffer for as you care so much about resolving this specific issue.
10. **Who do you want to help:** Sometimes the question is less about you and more about who. Is there a specific type of person or group of people who you really care about and want to support?
11. **Brainstorm:** Put pen to paper in your journal and write down ideas for who you want to help, and how you could potentially help them.

12. **What would you do for free:** If money was completely out of the equation, what is it that you would do day in and day out? Or what is it that you would do for free for the rest of your life in the service of others?

13. **Fuck 'em:** When you are trying to discover your unique purpose, you'll have all the naysayers around you saying how you can't possibly do it, or that you're stupid to think you could change the world. But your hunger to live a purposeful life will allow you to mute the S-H-I-T coming from the mouths of the ones who don't understand. Thank them for their feedback and do whatever the fuck you want anyway, because your purpose is what you were born for, and not what they asked for.

14. **Action plan:** Once you think you may have found your purpose, then start setting goals around what you ultimately want to achieve in the long run, and what you must achieve in the short term in order to get there.

15. **Write it down:** Respect your life's purpose by writing it down on paper and looking at it every single day. Use it as motivation and a reminder to keep you on track, and to keep you moving towards it on a daily basis.

16. **Give it time:** Discovering your purpose may not, and usually doesn't happen overnight. So be patient and enjoy the beautiful journey of self-discovery.

Remember that your life's purpose is unique to you, and it may evolve over time. It is not set in stone, so be open to change and remain true to your own values and passions. Embrace the wonderful journey that you are on and trust that you will discover your purpose along the way. This isn't usually an easy path, but it is so worth it.

Finding out what you want to do in life is just like visiting an all-you-can-eat food buffet restaurant... stay with me. What happens when you visit these types of restaurants? Well, you pay your one-time entry fee, and you are now free to grab a plate and fill it up with whatever you want, and also, as many times as you want too. The majority of you will firstly grab a plate full of everything that you know for certain you'll enjoy because of previous evidence or your previous experiences, but then you decide to try some things that you're not too sure on. Well, why wouldn't you as you've already paid your entry right? You courageously start by trying something that you've put off trying before to see if you actually like it or not, and then realise it wasn't as bad as you thought, and you'd even go as far as saying you enjoyed it. So now you've gained a bit more confidence you decide to start trying some more weird and wonderful foods, and by doing this you quickly start to gain results. You soon start realising the things you do enjoy, and the things you don't. Now all you do is stick with more of the dishes that you do like and want and have less of the others that you don't like or want. It's the exact same thing you should do in your life because the only way you're ever going to know if you really like something or not is to try it yourself. So go out there and start tasting the flavours of life.

CHAPTER CHALLENGE

Pull out your journal and write down the things that you would like to do and achieve during your lifetime. Let your mind think of all the things that you've always ever wanted to do, and all of the things that you've been really inspired to learn more about. I really suggest you look up number 13 which is the concept called ikigai and fill out your own version.

BELOW YOU'LL FIND SOME DIFFERENT WAYS OF DISCOVERING WHAT YOU WANT:

1. **Try S-H-I-T Out:** Exactly what you've just read about the food buffet restaurant. Go out there and try things out. What have you got to lose?

2. **If money wasn't an obstacle:** Imagine if you had unlimited funds to do whatever you like. What would you do FOR FREE in the service of others for the rest of your life?

3. **1 Year left:** God forbid you found out you only had 1 year left to live, but still needed to make money (legally) to cover your basic living needs. What would you do to earn an income?

4. **Hobbies/Passions/Interests:** What do you find yourself naturally doing in your free time, and what things do you always think about doing or trying. Is there a way of eventually monetising this?

5. **Assess your strengths:** What things are you really good at and know that you could help others to improve too?

6. **Values and beliefs:** What are some of the things that you feel really strongly about, and how doing more of that could really make a big difference in this world?

7. **Journaling:** The more you take action, the more you can take note of your different experiences and reflect on how they made you feel.
8. **Meditation/Visualisation:** Remember that what you think about you will bring about, so keep thinking positively on the things you would like to have in your life.
9. **Networking:** One of the best ways to find your purpose is to surround yourself with people who already know theirs. So, start surrounding yourself with individuals who know exactly what they want in life, and that clarity may well rub off onto you.
10. **Charity/Volunteering:** These roles usually have individuals help out because the greater cause is something that brings so much meaning to their lives, and also the lives of the ones receiving the support.
11. **Part time/free work:** If there is someone you know, or a company you like that are doing something you think you'd be interested in learning more about, then reach out and offer some spare time support in exchange for experience. Because you never know where it may take you.
12. **Previous challenges:** For many people a way of finding real meaning in their lives is to use the lessons they learned from facing and overcoming past pain in their own lives to then help others. This is because you already have the tools from going through those challenges yourself, and your ideal client is the individual who is currently in the same place as you once were. You can then share the story of how you overcame what you went through, and it will be used as a survival guide for someone else.

13. **Ikigai:** This is a Japanese concept that basically means 'reason for being'. You will find your own ikigai at the centre of the intersection between these four elements: What you love, what you're good at, what the world needs, and what you can be paid for. The idea behind ikigai is to find balance between these four elements to achieve purpose and fulfilment in life.

BONUS CHALLENGE
Sit somewhere peaceful with your journal and try and work out your unique ikigai.

Many people are so committed to their job that they become blind to their unhappiness, or they are blinded by the bills as they are only focused on their income, but you should never stay in an unfulfilling job just because of the money; you can always make more money, but you can never make more time. Consider taking a pay cut from your current unsatisfied salary to then be able to discover what gives you a true sense of purpose, meaning, and fulfilment.

Start living your life as if your life depends on it... Because it fucking does!

"It is in your moments of decision that your destiny is shaped."

SETTING YOUR G.P.S

If you don't have somewhere to head towards in life, then you're going to waste the majority of your time just drifting around. Imagine a boat that's out at sea which has no port of call. What's going to happen to that boat? It's going to sail around for days and weeks, or maybe even months and years whilst looking for something, anything, until it finally runs out of fuel, and when it does eventually run out, then it's down to the winds and tides to blow it in its chosen direction. Just know that it's the same winds which blow us all, and it's never too late to reset your sails!

I'm sure the majority of you have all used a G.P.S or Sat-Nav at some point throughout your life. The great thing about this piece of equipment is that all it needs is two pinpoint pieces of data to figure out your journey, which is where you currently are, and exactly where you want to be. I want you to imagine an aeroplane that's flying from London to New York. Before leaving, the pilot must know what airport they are currently stationed at, and also exactly which airport they will be flying into. Once the plane is up in the air then it will be put on autopilot. This will constantly measure and monitor the path towards its desired destination, and then make any necessary course corrections, if and when required. If at any moment the pilot needs to take back control of the aircraft to avoid turbulence etc, then the plane must be put back on to auto-pilot and the satellite navigation system must be checked. Imagine if the plane was now flying only just 1 degree out to the correct flight path it should be taking, over the course of just a handful more hours where could this plane end up? Who knows, Miami or Montreal!

Before racing off down your personal path of purpose, you must also set your own life's G.P.S and begin with the end in mind. This is because direction is way more important than speed. Think about it, if you don't clearly know where you're heading then you could be going 1000 MPH in completely the wrong direction. This is why you need to be super clear with your goals in life. Just the same as driving somewhere new. You need to be absolutely certain of two things, which are where you currently are in your life, and exactly where you want to be, and then any red lights, roadblocks, or wrong turns will be diverted. Because the G.P.S system will never say it's not possible to ever get there or tell you to go back home and just forget about it.

SOME OF THE BENEFITS OF HAVING CRYSTAL CLEAR CLARITY IN LIFE INCLUDE:
1. **Improved decision making:** Having a clear understanding of your values, goals, and priorities can help you make decisions that are aligned with what is most truly important to you right now.
2. **Increased focus:** Clarity allows you to focus your energy and resources on the things that matter most, which leads to better productivity and progress towards achieving your goals.
3. **Reduced stress:** When life feels uncertain or directionless your stress levels can rise as a result. However, having clarity can help reduce your stress by providing you with a clear path and a sense of purpose.
4. **Increased confidence:** Knowing what you want and ultimately how to achieve it can increase your self-confidence and self-esteem.
5. **Better relationships:** Clarity can also improve the relationships in your life because you are able to

effectively communicate your wants, needs, and boundaries.

6. **Enhanced well-being:** Having a clear understanding of your life purpose and direction can lead to greater overall happiness and well-being.

What is it that separates the 'average' person from the 'extraordinary' individuals?

G-O-A-L-S

Every single person who you look up to as 'successful' has undoubtedly set themselves a target to reach before setting out on a potential road to nowhere, and they all have had a clear definition of purpose in some way. I want to remind you that it's totally ok to not know your overall life's goal and purpose right in this moment, because life goals, visions, dreams, and purposes are likely to change from time to time. But the most important thing is that you're consciously and actively looking for what it is that you want and are making moves forwards to achieve it; the majority of people don't know what they want, and they never end up knowing. This is because they never sit down and do a simple exercise like putting a pen to paper and asking themselves the question "WHAT THE FUCK DO I WANT IN MY LIFE!" But the ironic thing is that every single one of them could tell you EXACTLY what they don't want. Just realise that the person with no dream, direction, or desired destination, is definitely determined to duplicate their daily deeds for an infinite duration.

I WOULD LIKE TO SHARE WITH YOU MY VERSION OF GOAL SETTING:

1. **Big 'hairy-ass' goal:** This goal is your overall gigantic life's goal. It's the one that seems unattainable and almost impossible. It's the one

that's scary AF. It's the one where people call you MAD, and it's the one that makes you start to question your own sanity. If or when you find yourself in a real S-H-I-T situation, this goal is the beacon of light in the future that's going to get you up and out of bed in the mornings to start moving towards it, because deep down inside of you, your soul is yearning to achieve this. Not only for your own satisfaction, but for the huge positive impact that you know achieving it would have on others.

2. **10 year challenge:** This is a vision that you could and should set yourself to start seeing what's possible, and what your life could really look like in a decade's time if you did decide to focus on continuous self-improvement and taking consistent steps forwards.

3. **5 year plan:** This is where you set yourself some scary, difficult, yet fully achievable goals with enough applied effort over a 5-year period. Come up with between 5 – 15 big goals that you believe you could conquer if you pushed yourself enough.

4. **Yearly goals:** Now I'm not talking about New Year's resolutions here at all. I'm talking about a specific goal, and there is a big difference... so let me explain. New Year's resolutions are personal promises that most people set themselves after Christmas leading into a new year to help improve or change something in their life, and the majority of people have already given up on these by the end of January. Yearly goals on the other hand are specific, measurable, and time-bound objectives which aim to achieve certain outcomes. While New Year's resolutions are often general and emotional, yearly goals tend to be more specific and practical.

5. **Quarterly goals:** Break your year up into 4x 90-day sections and set yourself specific targets to hit at each of the 4 different stages throughout the year. Doing this can help improve things like clarity, decision making, and time/task management.
6. **Monthly targets:** Monthly targets are a great stopping point between your weekly objectives and your quarterly goals. This is a great time to pause and to look back to see your achievements, make any adjustments, and start making improvements to achieve your quarterly goals.
7. **Weekly objectives:** Weekly objectives are great because they are in full visibility. You can clearly see your target at the end of each week and just need to take the required action on what it is that will get you over the finish line.
8. **Daily intentions:** You must wake up each day with intention, because if you don't then your precious 24-hour opportunity will soon pass you by. Realise that we all have the same 24 hours in a day, every billionaire, and every bum, but it's down to you to make the most out of your 86,400 single seconds. I personally like to set myself 3 goals each day and then highlight the 1 which is a non-negotiable and must be achieved no matter what.
9. **25 minute sprint:** The 'pomodoro' technique is a time management method that helps increase productivity and reduce distractions. I personally love to use this to achieve small goals throughout my day and find it really helps with things like reading and writing. The way it works is to pick a task, set yourself a 25-minute timer, and then focus only on the task in hand with absolutely no distractions or interruptions. After the 25 minutes

are up then reward yourself with a 5-minute break to get up, stretch, listen to your favourite music, or do something you enjoy. After those 5 minutes are up then repeat the process.

Don't look at this and get super overwhelmed but look at it as a way of breaking down the steps to achieving your dream life. Because if you think about it, this type of goal setting is literally the messy middle part between where you currently are and where you ultimately want to be.

Just know that all goals need three things:

DIRECTION
ACTION
TIME

Always remember to celebrate every mini milestone along the way by rewarding yourself. This could be in various different ways, and as simple as spending some time listening to your favourite music or taking yourself out to your favourite restaurant. The choice is completely yours, just make sure you do it as it triggers the reward centre within your brain and releases dopamine which is the feel-good chemical. Dopamine is the chemical of motivation and just like a drug, when released, your brain is always craving more, which in return (if used correctly) can help you to achieve great things in your life. Rewarding yourself will allow your brain to recognise, remember, and reinforce the reasons for why you should push yourself to then achieve the next challenge in the future.

Many people believe life is straight and smooth, however this is nothing but the opposite of the truth. I want you to think of something called the 'Tarzan theory'. When

Tarzan wants to go from one side of the jungle to the other, it is never a straight route as he must swing from vine to vine. Sometimes he goes left, other times he goes right, and sometimes he must first go backwards to then make progress forwards for the future. It's the same in your life, because there will be times you go left and times you go right, but there will also be those more challenging times when you need to assess where you currently are, and then make the decision whether going back briefly is going to be difficult in this current moment, but much better for you further in the future.

CHAPTER CHALLENGE

This exercise is going to require that you pull out your journal and set your own G.P.S which stands for Goal, Plan, See. It's vital to write this down on paper because when you do, you can then physically see your thoughts and plans in front of you, and then it makes it that much easier to understand, in return making it easier to figure out any potential problems you may be faced with. So anytime you're all up in your head overthinking certain thoughts or decisions, pull out your journal and literally think on paper.

1. **Goal:** Begin with the end in mind by setting your long-term target, because you can't hit a target that you can't see. Imagine watching a football match with no goals. The players would just be running around with nowhere to go and nothing to aim for!

2. **Plan:** This is the gap between where you currently are and where you want to be. You will never get to where you want to be by missing out on all of the messy middle part. I say the word 'messy' because you can't be too

solid with your plans. Things are always going to go differently to how you expect them to go, so you must be flexible. One day you'll go right, the next day you'll go left, and some days you'll find yourself going back, but don't stress too much because life is not linear, and this is a normal part of the growth journey; life is just like a game of chess. Sometimes you have to move backwards in order to then make better moves forwards, but as long as you've already set your goal then eventually the correct path will be presented.

3. **See:** Remember that every single thing which has ever been created has been created twice. That's once in the mind and once in reality. Every single day visualise what that dream life looks like within your own mind, and take a mental note of how you look, how you feel, plus the people and the things that are around you. By repeatedly doing this you are exercising and activating the Reticular Activating System within your brain which is the brain's filtering system.

Use this model to set your own G.P.S by clearly writing down your specific goal/s. Next write out and create a flexible plan for the potential steps you may take to eventually get there. Then use visualisation tools to get your mind focused on what it is that you want, the things you need to do to achieve it, and to also help attract the things you desire towards you. This could be in ways of meditation, vision boards, or even better to draw your own future!

"If you don't know where you're going then any road will get you there."

CHANGE BEGINS IN THE MIND

Whether you know it or not, you have designed an image of yourself within your mind, and also created a story about you and the world around you. The story you constantly tell yourself will make up your identity and dictate what you believe you can or can't achieve. The crazy thing is that many individuals are living a miserable life of mediocrity all because of the made-up story they have personally made within their own mind, and they have unconsciously created an identity/story which is totally opposite to the future that they ultimately want. The only way you can create the future which you desire, is to begin with first changing your identity. Because if you change your story, you can literally change your life.

Let's take someone who is a smoker for example. They may tell themselves something like, it's because their parents always smoked that is the reason for why they do it. Because of this, they hold on to that belief and the story they have made within their own mind, and they now put the blame on someone else. Just know that when you push the power to the external, it means that you have absolutely no control over it, and now it's not possible to change. You have to start owning your own S-H-I-T and start changing the way you talk to yourself, because your thoughts, feelings, and identity will dictate what you do or don't do. So anytime you notice negative thoughts, you need to replace them with positive and powerful ones which will then help elevate your self-belief.

You'll never surpass your own self-image because if you always think you're a specific type of person, whether it be it a smoker, a drinker, or even a procrastinator, then you're always going to identify yourself as that person, and that is who you will always be. But only until you make the decision to start thinking and acting in the ways which you imagine your future best-self to be will you achieve the life you truly want. Realise that your only limitations in life are the ones that you have personally created within your own mind.

BELOW ARE SOME OF THE BENEFITS OF UPGRADING YOUR OWN SELF-IMAGE:
1. **Increased confidence:** A positive self-image enhances your self-confidence, because when you believe in yourself and your own abilities, you are more likely to take on new challenges and approach them with a positive attitude.
2. **Improved relationships:** A healthy self-image allows you to have more fulfilling relationships with others. When you feel good about yourself, you are more likely to engage in healthier communication and set boundaries, leading to more authentic connections.
3. **Resilience:** A positive self-image makes you more resilient in the face of setback and challenges. You are better equipped to bounce back from failures and keep moving forward with determination.
4. **Better mental health:** A positive self-image is linked to improved mental well-being, because when you have a more positive view of yourself, you are less likely to experience feelings of anxiety, depression, or low self-esteem.
5. **Increased motivation:** Upgrading your self-image can fuel your motivation to achieve your goals and aspirations. When you believe in your capabilities,

you are more likely to pursue your dreams with enthusiasm.

6. **Productivity and success:** With an improved self-image, you are more likely to set higher goals and work persistently towards achieving them. This increased motivation and focus can lead to greater productivity and success in various areas of your life.

7. **Better decision making:** A positive self-image allows you to make decisions based on self-assurance and clarity rather than being driven by self-doubt or fear of failure.

8. **Healthier lifestyle choices:** When you respect yourself, you are more likely to make healthier lifestyle choices, such as engaging in regular exercises, maintaining a balanced diet, and prioritizing self-care.

9. **Increased happiness:** An upgraded self-image leads to a more positive outlook on life, resulting in increased overall happiness and life satisfaction.

10. **Enhanced communication skills:** When you feel more confident and secure in yourself, your communication skills tend to improve. You can express your thoughts and feelings more effectively, leading to better interpersonal relationships.

11. **Greater assertiveness:** A positive self-image enables you to be more confident when expressing your needs and desires, which can lead to increased respect for others and a stronger sense of self-advocacy.

12. **Reduced stress:** A healthy self-image can help reduce stress and anxiety, as you are less likely to

dwell on negative self-perceptions or worry excessively about what others think of you.

13. **Improved leadership abilities:** With an upgraded self-image, you are more likely to step into leadership roles and inspire others. Believing in your leadership abilities can positively influence your decision-making and ability to guide others.

CHAPTER CHALLENGE

You can make an identity shift at any given moment, and you can decide exactly who you want to be in this very instant. So, stop identifying yourself with past patterns, start eliminating disempowering habits from your life, and start replacing them with the habits which are going to contribute towards helping you evolve into the new and improved version of yourself. Pull out your journal and answer these questions below.

1. **What is the story you're currently telling yourself for why you can't achieve your goals?**
2. **What is the identity/story that you need, to become your very best self?**
3. **What do you need to start doing?**
4. **What do you need to stop doing?**
5. **What do you need to continue doing?**
6. **What one change can you start implementing today?**

Please realise that you can't build your dream on the exact same set of foundations on which you already created your nightmare.

"You can't become who you want by remaining who you are."

YOU ARE WHAT YOU REPEATEDLY DO

We as humans are all creatures of habit. Meaning a lot of our day to day lives are actually run on 'auto pilot'. For example, think of the last time you drove to work. Was it hard or easy to find your way there? I'm sure like the most of us you said it was super easy, and sometimes it's so familiar that we even say to ourselves we could do the complete journey with our eyes closed. But have you ever wondered why this is?

The reason for this is because the drive to work has become a habit of yours, and a habit is a routine behaviour which tends to happen without you even realising. We all have many habits, some good, others not so, and unknowingly we have been practicing these over and over again on repeat. By repeatedly practicing these habits, they have become deeply engrained within our minds. Think of it like this. Have you ever driven home from work and didn't even remember the journey? I mean you get home, and you think, "HOW THE FUCK DID I JUST GET HERE?" It's because you were so focused on everything else that's going on in your life that you didn't once think about driving your car, but somehow you still managed to arrive safely back at home.

Your brain is constantly churning throughout the day, so wants to save energy wherever possible and always wants to take the easiest route in life. It wants to take the path of least resistance which ultimately leads straight to pleasure. You could compare this to walking through an overgrown forest. Deep down you know where you want to get to, but because that part of the forest is so overgrown, you take the well-worn path that everybody else has taken, even though your pretty sure that it's not going to get you to where you want to be. Of course, it feels easy in the moment as you're happily strolling through the woodlands, but later down the line you realise that you're somewhere you really don't want to be in your life, but because you've been walking down that path for so long, it almost feels impossible to ever be able to change.

Replacing harmful habits with more beneficial ones is going to be hard, but just know that it isn't impossible. It takes time, dedication, and repetition, but most of all the desire to want to become better, because your desire to change MUST be greater than your desire to stay the same. Think back to that overgrown path where you know that your next level of life is waiting for you on the other side. The most difficult part is always going to be the first few steps to break through the barrier of change, but as long as you keep pushing forwards, you're going to build up momentum and that difficult path will start beginning to become that much easier to forge, because an object in motion usually stays in motion.

Charles Duhigg wrote the amazing book called 'THE POWER OF HABIT' which explains a concept called the 'habit loop'. The way Charles explains this is a bit like a computer program which consists of three parts.

THESE THREE PARTS OF THE HABIT LOOP INCLUDE:
1. **Cue:** This is a trigger that tells your brain to go into 'autopilot' mode and tells your brain which habit you should use. Triggers can come from many different things including people, places, even tastes and smells.

2. **Routine:** This is the specific activity or behaviour you perform after you are triggered. Some automatic routines can be great to unconsciously do throughout your day. However, others can actually be harmful for your personal growth and wellbeing.
3. **Reward:** This is what we gain from the habit, and it helps your brain understand if that particular loop is worth remembering for the future, then the reward will positively reinforce the action you took after you were first triggered.

EXAMPLE:

<u>SMOKING</u>
1. **Cue:** You feel stressed out and then see somebody smoking a cigarette. You smell the fumes, and suddenly want one yourself.
2. **Routine:** You proceed to light a cigarette and smoke it.
3. **Reward:** After smoking the cigarette, you now feel less stressed.

Realise that the stronger the craving, the stronger your desire will be to carry out that specific habit. Just know that your habits will shape you, so pay attention and identify your bad habits so you can then focus on replacing/building more empowering habits that will contribute towards helping you become the very best version of yourself. The way that you can change your bad habits is to interrupt the CUE – ROUTINE – REWARD cycle.

Your current habit is that every time you feel stressed out you light up a cigarette to help you feel better momentarily. I want you to really think if this kind of habit is helping you become the best version of you in the long run, and if it's not then it's time to break the cycle and replace your current routines and rewards. Below is another example of the same bad habit. Notice how the cue is still the same but the improved habit and reward is going to help you become better.

1. **Cue:** You feel stressed out notice somebody else smoking a cigarette. You suddenly smell the fumes, and then you want one yourself.
2. **Routine:** Instead of lighting a cigarette you decide to put on some relaxing music and go for a walk away from the smoke.
3. **Reward:** After walking you feel a lot less stressed, and you now feel like you have accomplished something which is going to be good for your mental and physical health, in return releasing dopamine which is the brain's reward chemical.

BELOW ARE SOME EFFECTIVE STEPS TO HELP YOU DEVELOP AND MAINTAIN POSITIVE HABITS:
1. **Start small:** Begin with simple, manageable habits that you can easily incorporate into your daily routine. Starting small allows you to build momentum and sets you up for success.
2. **Set clear goals:** Define specific, measurable, achievable, relevant, and time-bound (SMART) goals. Having a clear vision of what you want to achieve will give you direction and motivation.
3. **Create a routine:** Consistency is key when forming habits. Establish a daily or weekly routine that includes time for your positive habits, as this helps

reinforce the behaviour and makes it easier to stick with it.

4. **Track your progress:** Keep a record of your habit-building journey. Use a journal, app, or habit tracker to monitor your daily activities and progress, because seeing your improvements over time can be motivating.

5. **Stay accountable:** Share your goals with a friend, family member, or join a supportive community. Having someone to hold you accountable can help you stay on track during challenging times.

6. **Celebrate small wins:** Acknowledge and celebrate your achievements, even if they seem minor, because by rewarding yourself for sticking to your positive habits reinforces the behaviour and boosts your motivation.

7. **Stay positive and patient:** Building habits takes time, and it's normal to encounter setbacks, so be kind to yourself and avoid self-criticism. Focus on the progress you've made rather than dwelling on any slip-ups.

8. **Visualize success:** Imagine yourself successfully maintaining the positive habits you want to develop, because visualization can enhance motivation and make your goals feel more attainable.

9. **Replace negative habits:** Identify any negative habits that might be hindering your progress and work on replacing them with positive alternatives. This might require you to practice self-reflection and self-awareness.

10. **Practice self-discipline:** Developing self-discipline is crucial for building positive habits. Learn to resist immediate gratification, focus on

playing the long game, and stay committed to your long-term goals.

11. **Use habit stacking:** Combine new habits with existing ones to create a chain of activities. For example, if you want to meditate daily, do it right after brushing your teeth in the morning.

12. **Stay flexible:** Life is unpredictable, and there will be times when you might not be able to stick to your routine. Be adaptable and find ways to adjust your habits when necessary, without giving up on them completely.

Building positive habits in your life can be transformative and lead to long-term personal growth and happiness. Remember, building positive habits is an ongoing process, and it's okay to take things one step at a time. Be patient with yourself and keep pushing forward. Over time these habits will become a natural part of your life, in return leading to long lasting positive change.

BELOW ARE SOME BENEFITS OF BUILDING POSITIVE HABITS IN YOUR LIFE:

1. **Improved productivity:** Positive habits help you become more efficient and focused on your daily tasks, as they reduce procrastination and increase the likelihood of completing important activities on time.

2. **Enhanced overall well-being:** Developing positive habits related to exercise, nutrition, and self-care can lead to improved physical health, mental well-being, and emotional balance.

3. **Increased self-discipline:** As you practice discipline in one area of your life, it tends to spill

over into other aspects, leading to overall personal growth.

4. **Reduced stress and anxiety:** Positive habits can provide a sense of structure and control, reducing stress and anxiety levels. Consistent routines and a self-care practice can also create a calmer and more relaxed state of mind.

5. **Boosted self-confidence:** Successfully establishing positive habits can give you a sense of accomplishment and boost your self-esteem. This can lead to a more positive self-perception and increased confidence in your abilities.

6. **Better time management:** By incorporating positive habits into your daily routine, you become more organized and efficient with your time, leading to increased productivity and reduced time wasted on unproductive activities.

7. **Long-term goal achievement:** Positive habits keep you on track toward achieving your long-term goals, and consistent efforts in the right direction can lead to significant progress over time.

8. **Improved relationships:** Positive habits like active listening, empathy, and regular communication can enhance your relationships with others, leading to better social connections and a stronger support network.

9. **Increased focus and concentration:** Positive habits, such as meditation or regular breaks during work can improve your ability to concentrate and maintain focus on tasks, leading to better performance and outcomes.

10. **Enhanced mental clarity:** Positive habits can help you clear your mind from distractions and

unnecessary clutter, allowing you to think more clearly and make better decisions.

11. **Greater resilience:** Building positive habits helps you develop coping mechanisms and resilience. When faced with challenges, you are more likely to maintain a positive outlook and continue to move forwards through difficulties.

12. **Improved creativity:** Positive habits can stimulate creativity by providing a structured and encouraging environment for generating new ideas and solutions.

CHAPTER CHALLENGE

Realise that your habits are either making or breaking you. Everybody has and needs habits in their lives, because the 'good habits' serve a purpose which is to conserve that mental energy and space within your mind so that you can then focus on more important tasks. However, the 'bad habits' are slowly destroying you. You must let go of who you once were, and who you currently are, in order to evolve into the next best version of yourself. Because what got you here, will never get you there.

1. Pull out your journal and write down an average day in your current life. Focus on the things that you repeatedly do, then write down the patterns and habits that you notice you have. For example, smoking, drinking, and eating junk food.

2. Now go back in your mind to the previous challenge where you created your 'perfect' day and pay close attention to the habits which your best-self has. Write down each habit you imagine your future-self has. For instance, what does their morning routine

look like, what is their diet like (both physical and mental), and how do they speak to themselves.

- Now compare your current habits to your future habits and look for any potential positive/negative differences between each group whilst keeping in mind the person who you ultimately want to become in the future.
- Next look at each of your current habits and ask yourself the question, "By doing this, is it getting me closer to or further away from where I want to be?"

Now that you are aware of the habits you've identified to be detrimental to your personal growth and development, you can start to remove and replace them with ones which will be beneficial for becoming your best self in the future. Below is an example of how you can do this, and what you need to do to make them stick.

EXAMPLE:

CURRENT HABIT: Procrastinating
FUTURE HABIT: Action taker

1. **Start by determining your CUE:** What is it that's caused you to procrastinate?
2. **Question your current habit:** What is the benefit and what is the consequence of doing this repeated routine?
3. **Interrupt the cycle:** Instead of doing what you usually do after the specific cue, consciously make a pattern interrupt so you can switch it with something more empowering.

4. **Replace the habit:** What routine can you do differently to help you become better?
5. **Write it down:** e.g. - When I procrastinate - I will take an action step forwards - because it will give me a result which will then help me determine what I need to do next – and by sticking to my old habit of procrastinating – I will remain in the same position.

OR FOR THE PREVIOUS SMOKING EXAMPLE:

When I feel stressed out – I will go for a walk – because it will help clear my mind and allow me to chill out – and by sticking to my old habit of smoking a cigarette – I will eventually become ill and then be even more stressed out about my health.

<u>BONUS CHALLENGE</u>

Habit stacking: This involves building new habits by 'stacking' them onto existing habits, and using the habits you already have as triggers or cues for establishing new habits. By linking a new behaviour to an existing one, you create a chain of actions that can make it easier to stick to the new habit over time.

HERE'S HOW HABIT STACKING WORKS:
1. **Identify an existing habit:** Start by identifying a habit that you already do consistently as part of your routine. Examples could include, brushing your teeth, making a cup of coffee in the morning, or waking your dog.
2. **Pair it with a new habit:** Once you have your existing habit, decide on the new habit you want to establish. Make sure the new habit is small and

manageable, as it's easier to integrate into your routine.

3. **Create a clear statement:** Form a simple "If-Then" statement that links the existing habit with the new one. Examples could include, "After I brush my teeth, I will do 10 minutes of meditation," or "After I make my morning coffee, I will read 3 pages of a book."

4. **Repeat consistently:** Practice the habit stack consistently and over time the repetition and association with the existing habit will make the new behaviour more automatic and ingrained.

Now all you need to do is stick with the promise you told yourself which was to decide to become the very best version of yourself, and then overtime the compound effect will take place and these new and improved habits will eventually become automatic. Understand that the compound effect also works the opposite way too. So, if you've been constantly doing disempowering and potential negative habits for so long, then they would have built on top of each other and strengthened overtime.

Habit stacking can be an effective strategy for making positive changes in your life and building a routine that supports your goals. It leverages the power of existing habits to create a foundation for new habits, making the process of behaviour change more manageable and sustainable. The key to successful habit stacking is to start with small, achievable habits and gradually build on them. As you gain momentum and feel more comfortable with the habit stack, you can add more complex or longer habits. The ultimate goal is to create a chain of positive behaviours that become a natural part of your daily life.

Know that it's repetition that is the mother of all skill, because nobody ate one burger and became unhealthy, just as nobody went on one run and became super fit. You need to practice your new habits every single day because practice doesn't make perfect, but practice does make progress and eventually makes permanent. Many people let the need for perfection stop them from progressing by procrastinating and not taking any further actions towards their dreams. You need to realise that done is better than perfect. Your job is not to become perfect, but to be better than you used to be. Focus on progress and not perfection because perfection doesn't exist, and why would anyone want to be perfect anyway because surely that means there is no more room for growth? In life it's progress that equals happiness. Real success doesn't come from what you just do occasionally, but from what you do consistently; losers do occasionally, what winners do daily. If you want to win in life then it will require courage and commitment, and also the discipline to do what is required, regardless of whether you want to do it or not.

"It's not what
we do once
in a while
that shapes our
lives but it's
what we do
consistently."

YOUR SURROUNDINGS SHAPE YOU

You become the average of the 5 people who you spend the most time with. If you constantly surround yourself with 5 smokers, then you're most likely to become the 6th. However, by spending the majority of your time with 5 millionaires for instance, then you're also most likely to become the 6th. This may sound a little crazy, but it's true. Because over time you unconsciously start to replicate the traits and habits of the ones you surround yourself with the most. This is why it's vital to surround yourself with people who are preforming at the top of their game, and with those who are constantly pushing their limits to level up their lives to become the very best versions of themselves. Because if you surround yourself with 3's and 4's for too long, then the 5's and 6's start looking really good. But by repeatedly surrounding yourself with 9's and 10's its likely to rub off on you, and as a result you'll find yourself wanting to also level up your life.

Remember that you get to choose the places you go, the people you interact with, and the content you consume. You are the C.E.O of your life and certain people around you will need to be fired, and others must be hired. If you look at your circle and aren't inspired or empowered to better your life, then you don't have a circle, but you have a cage. So, surround yourself with winners, doers, believers, and achievers, because that way you will unintentionally be forced to level up your life. Get away from the gossipers because if they are talking crap about other people behind their backs, then you better fucking believe that they won't think twice about talking S-H-I-T about you when you're not there.

When you are walking on your path of purpose you better keep an eye out for the dream stealers, the doubters, the haters, and the put-me-fucking-downers, because people are either like vacuums or like chargers. The vacuums will suck the energy and the drive out of you, in return holding you back. However, the chargers will help boost you up to your next level of life. You get to choose whether you have expanded or limited association with certain individuals, and if particular people in your life are like energy vampires, then you should really consider disassociation. It comes to a point in your life where you must make the decision, to make an incision, and cut them out of your life. I know this sounds difficult and that's because it is, but surrounding yourself with negative people just because you've known them for a long time, or because that's what you've always done is like trying to drag a 10-ton weight on your back whilst climbing your own ladder of life. It's not going to make your journey impossible, but it's going to make it so much harder. You're going to start feeling like a great white shark who's been put in a pond, and this is because you've started to outgrow certain people, places, and situations. You need to make the solid decision of who you surround yourself with, and those who you allow a premium access pass into your precious life, because if they can't grow with you, then they can't go with you!

I know you're thinking S-H-I-T because some of these people are good friends or even family members. Look, I'm not suggesting that you stop speaking to your family and cut yourself off from all your friends, but to be extremely mindful about who you're spending your time with, and who you're allowing access to your precious energy. If you find yourself in disempowering environments, then make the decision to remove yourself from those environments and then become 'unavailable'. What do I mean by this? Well, if you're going to places where you know for certain that there are energy vampires feeding and breeding there, then make the decision to remove yourself from those environments and if/when they ask why you aren't showing up anymore, then tell them that you have other priorities. Realise that you can't change the *people* around you, but you can change the people *around* you. So, start surrounding yourself with people who fit your future and not your past, because it comes to a point in your life where your circle decreases in size but increases in value.

I've once believed I could change the people around me by telling them what I think they should do, but all this does is create massive resistance to change and actually has a totally opposite effect. Think of it this way, you can either act like a tow boat or a lighthouse. Both ways are aiming to achieve the same results, which is to get the stranded boat back into the safety of the harbour. However, each way has a completely different approach to one and other. The tow boat races out to the stressed ship, hooks up a winch, and then battles to drag it back in to shore with extreme force. The lighthouse stays rooted tall in position and shines its bright beacon of light out to sea to then light the way and guide the boat back to safety. Of course, each way could work, but by using the tow boat method it's going to take a lot more time and energy. It's the same in life. When you try to force change on someone, they will instantly feel threatened and put their guard up, in return wanting to distance themselves from you. Understand that you should never try and force change on somebody else because true change always starts with self. It starts with you being the change that you want to see in the world, and then being a role model to others by becoming the very best version of yourself. By doing it this way, you will start to attract the right kind of people into your life. Realise that you can lead a horse to water, but you can't make it drink. However, you can show the horse the benefits of drinking that water by drinking it yourself on a daily basis.

Surroundings are vital because you could be in the 'worst place' of your life but have amazing people around you and things will seem to sort themselves out much quicker. But the same is true for the opposite. You could be in the 'best place' of your life but be surrounded by negative people and you soon notice things start turning S-H-I-T. This is why it's so important to surround yourself with likeminded positive people who are also heading in the same or similar directions to you. All it takes is to spend a little bit too much time in the wrong crowd to then feel the force of their negativity weighing down on your life. Know that you are a product of your environment, but your environment can also be a product of you.

When you begin to break out of the box that society has tried to keep you trapped in for so long, and when you start to go after the things that you really want to do, then you're going to soon have certain individuals talk S-H-I-T about you and they'll say things like, "Who the fuck do they think they are?" As soon as you notice this then you need to realise that these aren't your people, and that you need to get away from them as quick as you fucking can. This is only said by people who are jealous of you, who want to see you fail, and those who don't have your best interest at heart. Realise that your haters actually hate themselves for not having the courage to do what you're doing. That's why it's so important to surround yourself with the people who not only want you to become your best, but also support you in helping you become your very best. With this being said, you need to understand that its ok to love your friends and family from a distance. It doesn't mean that you don't love them, it just means that you love and respect yourself more.

You also need to ask yourself if you are surrounded by actual friends or just fans. This is because you will most likely have certain individuals around you who act like your 'fans' as they cheer and support everything you do whatever the result. Obviously, this is nice, however, you need to watch out as these types of people sometimes won't help you in pushing through the barriers to reach the new and improved version of yourself. True friends on the other had will hold you accountable for the things you said you were going to do, they will challenge you to become better, and they will always call you out on your S-H-I-T. You must have a handful of true friends around you who will let you know when you're slipping as they are the ones who will make sure you stay on track to eventually achieve your goals.

CHAPTER CHALLENGE

This challenge may feel pretty S-H-I-T but it is totally necessary in order for you to maintain your mental health and well-being, and to also make more empowering changes to help level up your life. Take a look at your current surroundings and then ask yourself the honest question, whether the individuals around you are supporting or suffocating your success.

BELOW ARE SOME WAYS HOW YOU CAN START ELIMINATING NEGATIVE PEOPLE FROM YOUR LIFE:

1. **Identify the negative people:** It's so important to be totally honest with yourself and sit down with your journal to identify the negative people in your life. Write a list of the individuals who are constantly putting you down, doubting your abilities, and overall making you feel real S-H-I-T about yourself.

2. **Set boundaries:** Once you have identified those negative people then it's very important to set your own boundaries with them. Depending on the severity of their negativity you can choose to limit the amount of time you spend with them, avoid certain conversations, or even decide to end specific relationships all together.

3. **Surround yourself with positivity:** Choose to focus on good vibes only. This means putting yourself in places with great energy and supportive people who will ultimately help raise you up to your next level of life.

4. **Practice self-care:** When you find yourself in toxic environments it can be extremely tiring to keep up with the constant challenges, and it can also be so easy to begin beating yourself up within your own mind. If it isn't possible to get away from these people and out of these places straight away, then make sure you give yourself a break from it by engaging in activities that bring you joy, and to also practice things like journaling, walking, and meditation to help clear your mind and reduce your stress levels.

5. **Seek support:** If you're finding it overwhelming and really difficult to deal with or to move away from, then it may be beneficial to seek support from a trusted friend, family member, or mental health professional.

You have to prioritise your health and happiness, because if you don't then the energy vampires will suck you dry, and you'll find it difficult to do anything to benefit yourself. So, stay away from negative people as they have a problem for every solution. If someone or something is getting in the way of your progress in a relationship, your career, health, or happiness then you need to start making rapid changes. Remember that it's ok to distance yourself from those types of people even if they are close friends or family members, because anything in life that costs your mental health is already way too expensive!

"Proximity
is
power."

KNOW WHEN IT'S TIME TO LEAVE

Know your fucking worth and then add tax. If you don't know your own value, then someone else will decide it for you and it will always be a lot less than what you're actually worth. Don't let others keep putting a discounted price tag on your skills and abilities and realise that your value doesn't ever decrease because of somebody else's inability to see your worth!

Self-worth is defined as the level of importance one places on themselves. It is a fundamental part of your being and controls the way you see yourself. To most people, self-worth only comes after achieving something that is greater than another individual's achievements. The fact is that life isn't about being in competition with anybody or being seen to be better than someone else. The only person you should ever be in competition with is yourself, so you can then focus on becoming a better version of who you once were. The number of friends and followers you have, your job title, or the digits in your bank account don't determine how much you're worth as an individual, so stop measuring your self-worth using someone else's ruler. If you find yourself constantly trying to prove your worth to someone, then you've already forgotten your own value. Sometimes we try to show the world that we are flawless in the hope of being liked and accepted by everyone, but you can't please everyone, and you shouldn't event try to. You don't have to put on a mask and pretend to be someone who you're not, because you have nothing to prove to anyone else. Know that the people worth impressing just want you to be yourself; what may impress one person may not impress another. Focus on impressing yourself and you will then attract the right kind of people towards you who deserve your time. Remember that the only person you need to impress is you!

If you ever find yourself in places or situations where you don't feel listened to, respected, understood, or valued then get the fuck out. Learn to respect yourself and walk away from any friendship or relationship that isn't serving you or that doesn't feel right. You have literally one opportunity at this gift of life, so don't waste your days trying to convince people of your true value and worth. The wrong people will always think you are S-H-I-T even when you know that you're at your very best. However, the right people will think you're an absolute gem even when you know that you're at your very worst. Think of it this way. A big bottle of water is £0.75 at the supermarket, £1.50 at the gym, £3 at the cinema, and £4.50 on an aeroplane. It's the exact same water, but the only thing that changed its value is the place where it was sold. So next time that you're feeling 'worth less' then maybe you're just in the wrong place. Put yourself in environments that bring out the best in you, and environments where you are encouraged to thrive.

If you are sat in a room that stinks of S-H-I-T then it's going to be super uncomfortable because it smells disgusting at first, but over time you start to normalise that unpleasant smell and it becomes much more tolerable as time passes by. As the smell gets weaker and weaker, you then start to accept that S-H-I-T smell as the norm and decide to stay put. This is the same for certain people and places in your life. You may have found yourself in an undesirable situation where you know deep down that you shouldn't stay, however, you chose to stay and end up brainwashing yourself into believing things aren't too bad, and that they will get better, but the reality is that they are constantly getting worse. If you notice that you've been stuck in a crappy environment for quite some time, then make the decision to start removing yourself from those places. Of course, it may not be possible to make massive instant changes, but you can take instant action steps to start planning out what you're going to do over the coming days, weeks, and months ahead.

Leaving toxic environments might not always be easy, especially if they involve personal relationships or work situations. However, prioritizing yourself and making conscious choices to surround yourself with positivity can lead to significant improvements in various aspects of your life. So being aware of your surroundings and then consciously choosing to remove yourself from those negative or toxic environments can help improve your physical, mental, and emotional well-being.

BELOW ARE SOME OF THE BENEFITS OF BEING AWARE OF YOUR SURROUNDINGS:
1. **Improved mental health:** Toxic environments can take a toll on your mental health, leading to increased stress, anxiety, and even depression. But, by distancing yourself from such environments, you allow yourself the space to heal and reduce the negative impact on your mind.
2. **Enhanced emotional well-being:** Toxic environments often involve negative emotions, conflicts, and unhealthy dynamics. Removing yourself from these situations can create a more positive and emotionally stable space for yourself, allowing you to experience greater happiness and contentment.

3. **Increased productivity:** Toxic environments can be distracting and draining, making it difficult to focus and be productive. By surrounding yourself with positivity and support, you create an atmosphere conducive to achieving your goals and being more efficient.

4. **Healthy relationships:** Toxic environments tend to foster unhealthy relationships that can be damaging to your self-esteem and overall happiness. Removing yourself from these situations allows you to seek out healthier, more supportive relationships that uplift and inspire you.

5. **Physical health benefits:** Chronic stress and negativity can have adverse effects on your physical health, contributing to issues like headaches, insomnia, and a weakened immune system. By leaving toxic environments, you reduce the likelihood of these health problems.

6. **Increased self-awareness:** Being aware of your surroundings and recognizing toxic elements helps you develop greater self-awareness. You become more attuned to your own emotions, boundaries, and needs, enabling you to make more conscious decisions about your life.

7. **Personal growth:** Leaving negative environments forces you to adapt and grow, as it challenges you to explore new opportunities, learn from past experiences, and develop resilience in the face of adversity.

8. **Better decision making:** When you are consciously aware of your surroundings, you are more likely to make informed and rational decisions rather than being influenced by negative peer pressure or toxic behaviour.

9. **Enhanced creativity:** Positive environments that foster support and encouragement can boost your creativity and innovation. When you feel safe and inspired, you are more likely to think outside the box and explore new ideas.
10. **Increased happiness and fulfilment:** Ultimately, removing yourself from negative environments and choosing positivity allows you to experience greater happiness and fulfilment in life. This is because you are more in control of your own well-being and can actively shape your reality in a positive way.

CHAPTER CHALLENGE

This week, pay close attention to your surroundings and keep notes in your journal every single day of how they made you feel, then at the end of the week review what you've recorded and put each specific environment into one of three categories:

1. **Limiting environments:** These are places which limit your personal growth and happiness. (This could be spending excessive amounts of time with pessimistic minded friends or family members) **Spend less time in these environments.**

2. **Progressive environments:** These are places which contribute to your overall well-being and self-development (This could be a networking group or club of people who share similar hobbies and interests) **Spend more time in these environments.**

3. **Toxic environments:** These are places which drain your energy levels completely (This could be spending any amount of time with people who treat you like absolute S-H-I-T) **Completely remove yourself from these environments.**

Understand that certain people in your life aren't loyal to you, but they are loyal to their need of you. However, once their needs change then so does their loyalty. The truth is you never really know somebody until they don't get what they want, and that is when they will show their true colours. If someone does show you their true colours, then never try to repaint them and whatever you do, don't try to convince yourself that you're colour blind! With this being said, you need to make sure you are always looking out for wolves disguised in sheep's clothing, and as soon as you do notice that something isn't right, then it probably isn't so you need to get the fuck away fast.

"Nobody cares
about your life
as much as
you do."

SELF-CARE ISN'T SELFISH

Self-care is essential for living a healthy and happy life, and by prioritising your own self-care, you can improve both your physical and mental well-being. Regular self-care practices can include anything from exercise and healthy eating, all the way to mindfulness and meditation. By frequently practicing self-care you can really focus on and start to understand your own wants and needs. You are also able to begin improving your ability to make the best use of your time and energy both effectively and efficiently, which will ultimately lead to increased productivity and overall success in all areas of life.

You need to set clear boundaries with people, and you need to put a price on your precious time. Anything that doesn't meet the value of your own worth should be limited and eventually eliminated. You must put yourself first in life, because if you don't then other people will rob you of your time and energy, which will ultimately be harmful to your overall health and happiness. You have to figure out what you want in your life and then limit your exposure to the things that aren't that. If you don't have any boundaries for your life and you accept the S-H-I-T from other people, then you are teaching them exactly how you want to be treated, because in life we all get what we tolerate. However, when you stick to your own solid set of boundaries, you'll soon notice certain people start disappearing from your life, but look at this as solid evidence that those boundaries you set were needed. Daring to set boundaries is about having the self-respect and courage to put yourself, your priorities, and your needs first, even at the cost of potentially disappointing and not meeting the needs of others.

It's like when you're flying on an aeroplane, and they say in the safety announcements before take-off, "In the event of an emergency you MUST put your own mask on first before assisting others." The reason they say this isn't because they want you to be selfish and not give a S-H-I-T about anyone else, but they want you to be momentarily selfish so in return you could potentially be selfless and have the ability to then help others. Because if you aren't running at full capacity in your life, then how the fuck are you going to be able to assist others who are demanding energy from you?

Your energy is priceless, so treat it as if it was like the money in your bank account. Budget it, save it, and find different ways to increase it. Invest it where you know you'll get a good return on time-investment and realise that your energy is your true currency. Compare it to a fully charged battery. Most days you begin with 100% capacity. However, with each task throughout the day your battery level is reduced. Let's say just going to work for the day alone would take up 60-70% of your energy levels, but the more you expose yourself to energy draining environments, the less you'll have for other more important tasks. For instance, every negative conversation you engage in, every moment spent scrolling social media looking at S-H-I-T, and every negative thought you hold on to within your own mind are just some examples of the things that will significantly reduce your energy levels during your day. But there are also many different ways of replenishing your charge too.

BELOW ARE JUST A FEW WAYS IN WHICH YOU CAN HELP BOOST YOUR ENERGY LEVELS:

1. **Morning routine:** How you start you morning will completely shape your entire day, so start your day off with energy boosting activities which could include meditation and physical activity.

2. **Socialising:** Spending time having positive conversations both in person and online is vital to maintain and boost your energy levels throughout the day.

3. **Taking breaks:** It's impossible to be at full throttle throughout the day and not run out of fuel, so taking short breaks to get up, stretch, and walk around is super important to not burn out. Remember the pomodoro technique from previous chapters, which is a solid 25 minutes focused solely on one task, and then a 5-minute break to reward yourself.

4. **Mindfulness:** You can do this from anywhere, and one simple example is to close your eyes, do some deep breathing, and try to clear your mind. This is a great way to slow down your brain and help reduce energy consuming stress levels.

5. **Sleep:** This is the most important part of recharging and replacing the energy that's been drained throughout the day. You must obtain the necessary amount of uninterrupted sleep you need in order to recharge your battery to 100%. Some ways to help you achieve this is to create yourself a night-time routine where you begin winding down an hour before you want to sleep. You can do this by meditating or reading, removing all electronic devices, and making sure your room is as dark as possible.

Another important part of self-care is to ask for help when you need it. Asking for help isn't a sign of weakness, but in fact it's a huge sign of strength. It takes such strength to be willing to open up and admit that you are in need of help, and that you are willing to accept assistance from someone else who is more qualified in the specific area which you are currently struggling with. Know that life can sometimes be very difficult and it's hard to try and figure S-H-I-T out all by yourself. Realise that when you ask for help in any area or your life, you then create a space for others to exercise their helpfulness.

WAYS IN WHICH YOU CAN PRIORITISE YOUR HEALTH AND HAPPINESS:
1. **Set your standards:** You MUST set yourself a level of standards for your life and say NO to everything that doesn't meet those specifications, because if you don't then you'll find yourself letting things slip time and time again, to the point where you're not creating the life of which you dream and desire.
2. **Know your priorities:** Take some time to identify your values and reflect on what really matters most in your life, as this will help you prioritise where you spend your time and focus your energy.
3. **Schedule time for yourself:** You need to literally block out time for yourself in your calendar and make it non-negotiable.
4. **Set solid boundaries:** It's so important to set your own boundaries with people, and also share what your commitments are by clearly communicating with others. Your time and energy are the most valuable things you'll ever own.

5. **Say NO more:** Saying no to things that don't align with your priorities allows you to create space for the things that do. By saying no to someone else, you are actually saying yes to yourself!
6. **Practice self-care:** Take care of your physical, mental, and emotional well-being by engaging in energy preserving and enhancing activities that help you rest, relax, and recharge.
7. **Evaluate your commitments:** Check the commitments and activities in your life and determine if they are in alignment with your priorities, dreams, and desires, then start deciding whether you begin letting go of certain things that no longer support and serve you.
8. **Ask for help:** Don't be afraid to ask for help when you need it, because asking for support and guidance is a strength and not a weakness. It's ok to not be ok, but it's not ok to *stay* not ok.

Start by setting standards for your life and understanding the things that you want to prioritise. Your standards are the bare minimum levels of things that you will accept into your life from yourself and from the others around you. One of the greatest acts of self-care is to not go back to the things that once caused you tremendous pain, whether this is in a job, friendship, or romantic relationship just because it's familiar, and that you perceive it to be easy and comfortable in this current moment.

CHAPTER CHALLENGE

You only have one life so why wouldn't you prioritise yourself? You can't pour from an empty cup. Of course, it's important to be kind, generous, and supportive towards people, but never forget that you are 'people' too! You must have a specific level of standards for all areas of your life, because the standards you set determine the life you get, and the moment you do raise your required standards, is the moment you begin to level up your life.

Pull out your journal and write down the standards that you want to set for your life, then fill out your calendar for the week and make sure you time-block your priorities and self-care routines.

EXAMPLE: **STANDARDS**

STANDARDS FOR OTHERS – The type of people who you want to surround yourself with, and the level of S-H-I-T you're willing to take before you have to move away from them.	"I will only spend time with people who are positive thinkers, who give me constructive criticism, and add to my overall growth and well-being."
STANDARDS FOR YOURSELF – How will you show up for yourself and the people around you, and how will you treat yourself both physically and mentally?	"I will follow through with every goal which I have set for my health, wealth, happiness, and overall development. I will prioritise my wants and needs and also stick to my self-care schedule."
STANDARDS FOR YOUR FINANCES – How will you make, spend, and save your money?	"I am currently working in a 9-5 job and am planning to make the transition to leave my job next year and create a social media marketing company. In

	order to do this, I choose to sacrifice spending money on unnecessary things. I am now investing in online courses and mentors, and I am also building up a pot to cover 6 month's worth of expenses for when I do take the leap."

These are just some examples, but feel free to create and use your own. You should review your standards on a frequent basis to make sure they are still up to the quality of life you want to have for yourself and that they are still valid. This could be reviewed every 90 days for instance, and then re-written and hopefully raised every year.

Always remember that you cannot give what you do not have. You have to be BEAUTIFUL in order to help others, because trying to give to others when you cup is half full will only result in hardship. 'BE YOU TOO FULL' and help others only from your overflow, and don't let other people's problems become your priorities. True freedom begins when you STOP trying to meet other people's wants, needs, and expectations and START setting and sticking to your own goals, values, and boundaries. Never let someone else's false emergency become your main priority, because when you've set your own boundaries, and when you know your own standards you'll always put your own priorities first, stop giving a S-H-I-T about what others think of you, and you now understand that you are living your life to a level that is sufficient to first meet your own wants and needs.

"Always look after number one."

SACRIFICE FOR SUCCESS

You need to start letting things go that are currently weighing you down to be able to then begin levelling up in all areas of your life, and to also start becoming your best self. If you don't sacrifice for what you want, then what you want becomes the sacrifice. Realise that the greater your current pain, the greater the sacrifice, and greater the action steps will be required in order to change.

So many of you are sleeping on your fucking dreams. You wake up in the morning and hit snooze on your alarm, but by doing that I want you to know that you are doing a disservice not only to yourself, but also to the others around you, because one day you won't have the choice to press snooze, because that day you'll be snoozing forever. When you have a mission to achieve in your life, you won't need to set an alarm ever again as your soul knows that you only have limited time to make this vison a reality, so your internal alarm clock will always wake you up each day instead. Stop lying in bed oversleeping and start waking up earlier to create the life which you desire, rather than just dreaming about it. Imagine if I told you that you could be well on your way to designing and living your dream life within a handful of months/years, but only if you woke up just one hour earlier and dedicated that 'oversleeping time' to your goals instead. That's one hour per day and 7 hours in one week. We all have the same 168 hours in a week, and you're telling me you can't sacrifice 7 hours of oversleeping for 7 hours building your future?

Remember that whatever got you here will never ever get you there. You must sacrifice who you once were and who you currently are in order to evolve into the person who you dream and desire to be. You have to literally 'kill off' the old version of you to be able to blossom, bloom, and become the new and improved version of yourself. You'd be crazy to think that you're going to carry on doing the same old S-H-I-T over and over again, and then get different results. So many are saying that they want to create their dream life, but they don't fucking realise that if nothing changes, then nothing changes!

BELOW IS A LIST OF THINGS YOU MAY CONSIDER LETTING GO OF TO THEN MAKE SOME SPACE FOR THE THINGS THAT YOU DO WANT AND NEED:

1. **Time-wasting activities:** This could be anything from watching S-H-I-T on TV, to aimlessly scrolling social media.
2. **Unhealthy habits:** The obvious ones are things like overeating crap, smoking, and drinking. These harmful habits will all negatively impact your physical and mental health.
3. **Negative relationships:** You have to move away from draining relationships whether it's toxic friends, difficult family members, work colleagues, or even constantly complaining partners. Because if you don't then you will soon be consumed by their crap.
4. **Material possessions:** Start looking at all the S-H-I-T you own and start getting rid of the things you aren't using any more. You can easily start selling things online, or if you want to feel really good, then start donating some of your stuff to charity and let others benefit from your unused items.
5. **Social media detox:** I believe it's vital to de-clutter your social media from time to time (every quarter) to sift the S-H-I-T and unfollow the people and

pages that don't align with your own values, or that don't contribute to your overall growth and development.

6. **Overcommitting yourself:** Avoid 'shiny penny syndrome' by not saying "Yes" to everything and starting to say NO more. This will help prevent stress, overwhelm, and frustration.

7. **Procrastination:** Never put off until tomorrow what can be done today because tomorrow may never come. Stop fearing taking the first step and let go of your self-doubt as this is what's preventing you from achieving your future dreams. Yes, the first step is always the most daunting, but believe me when I say that its always the most rewarding.

8. **Negative self-talk:** Be very careful how you are speaking to yourself within your own mind as YOU are always listening. Always speak to yourself with kindness and encouragement, just like you'd speak to a struggling friend or family member.

9. **Approval from others:** Let go of the need for confirmation from others because nobody knows what's best for you, better than you; only you can truly know deep down inside. If you don't go within then you'll end up going without.

10. **Excuses:** Stop justifying your S-H-I-T excuses in your own mind for why you can't be, do, and have anything and everything you want in your life.

Sacrificing the old you to make space to start creating the new and improved you can sometimes be very hard, but you must realise that it's necessary and can also be incredibly rewarding down the line. It requires commitment to prioritise and focus on what matters most, to demonstrate discipline, and to also make many difficult choices, but by doing so you may be able to achieve your greatest goals and go on to live a life of fulfilment and abundance. Just know that you'll never become who you want by remaining who you are. The word 'sacrifice' has a very negative connotation around it, so let's replace it with 'investment in self' because self-investment is by far the best investment you'll ever make.

HERE ARE SOME WAYS WHICH YOU CAN START SACRIFICING/INVESTING IN YOURSLEF:

1. **Identify your priorities:** You should now know the importance of prioritising the things that matter most to you. Understand that you can't manage your time, but you can manage your tasks, so look at your daily/weekly/monthly list of the things that you will prioritise in your life and then focus mainly on them.

2. **Put in the work:** Success requires commitment, sacrifice, and hard work, so be prepared to work long hours and give up wasting your free time doing S-H-I-T. Only then can you put in the necessary amount of applied effort in order to achieve what it is that you really want. What comes easy doesn't last and what lasts doesn't come easy.

3. **Give up bad habits:** You can't carry on doing the same old S-H-I-T every day and expect things in your life to change for the better. You need to let go of those bad habits which are currently restricting your growth and holding you back from achieving success. Things like binging out on Netflix series and constantly filling your mind with S-H-I-T on TV, to always eating crap food and drinking your choice of poison on the weekends. Realise that plain people prioritise pleasure and the mediocre focus on

the media. Because they always put play first, and this is the exact reason the masses stay stuck in the mundane.

4. **Stay on track:** It can be so easy to give in to temptation or to give up completely when times get tough. Just know that it's discipline which is the bridge between your goals and accomplishments. A great way to avoid temptation is to design your environment by removing all temptations, because if it's out of sight then it's usually out of mind too. Understand that you will fuck up every once in a while, however, don't be too hard on yourself, learn from your mistakes and become stronger for next time.

5. **Reward yourself:** It's going to be difficult and also sometimes extremely challenging to sacrifice your old actions without wanting to turn around and go back to where you began from time to time. This is the reason for why you MUST reward yourself by celebrating all the mini milestones along the way. If you've finished a really big task that was on your list then you could reward yourself with a movie, or if you've done a smaller task, you could reward yourself by listening to some of your favourite music etc. It's super important to do this because it's what's going to give you the drive to then start and complete your next task. If you don't reward yourself for the work you've done, then you have absolutely no incentive to go on and do it again.

Society defines success as a safe and secure job whether you enjoy it or not, having a mortgage on a house, leasing a brand-new car, getting married, and having a couple of kids. Plus, for good measure if you don't achieve all this by the time you are 30 then you're looked at as a loser. Society is constantly putting so much pressure on young adults to become this carbon copy, cardboard cutout that's been created from social media's costly catalogue, and it's brainwashing the youth into believing that they are worthless unless they are fully dressed in designer brands, flashing Rolex watches on their wrists, or constantly cruising around in supercars.

DON'T BELIEVE ANY OF THIS S-H-I-T AND DON'T FALL INTO THIS TRAP!

The true meaning of success is exactly what you say it is and not what society says. Society's version of success can have you chasing S-H-I-T you don't really need to impress people you don't really like, in return keeping you trapped on the treacherous treadmill of life desperately trying to obtain thousands of things. Without even realising it, you've adopted the dissatisfied mindset of, "I'll be happy when…" whilst constantly chasing crap like cars, clothes, and careers. If you're living a life of lack with the materialistic mindset of, "I'll be happy when…" thinking things will make you fully fulfilled, then you need to think again because true happiness is not found in an item, person, or a place, but it is actually a way of life. If you believe someone or something other than you is going to make you truly happy, then you're going to miss out on the most important part of life which is this magical moment right now. This is because true happiness is homemade. You will never find it in someone or something else, so stop looking for external happiness and start searching internally because happiness is an inside job.

You need to make the rock-solid decision that you are going to create a meaningful life for yourself, and not one to try and impress anybody else. So many people are trying to make a made-up materialistic 'insta' lifestyle whilst trying to impress everyone else, rather than working to create a purposeful life to actually impress themselves. Nowhere in society's marvellous manual does it say to, "just be happy," so you need to define what the word success means to you and don't let others try and convince what you believe isn't right.

You don't have to go down the same path as everybody else, it's totally ok and necessary to create your own path in life, and if you want to be successful then start doing the opposite to the masses. The person who follows the crowd will only go as far as the crowd goes, however, the one who walks alone will find themselves in places not many have ever been or will ever be. Society says that we should have our whole lives figured out by the 'dreaded' age of 30, and that we should have a 'secure' job, be married, have a mortgage, a few kids, and also a car on finance. Understand that this stigmatized age is not when life is over. Life only ends at 30 if you choose to let it, and the people who are telling you that you must have your whole life planned out by 'the big 30' are giving you S-H-I-T advice, because they probably let life stop for them at that age. Of course, it would be good to have some things figured out by then, but don't ever let someone else convince you that your age is your cage. Yes 30 is a 'best before' date but it's not a fucking 'USE BY' date. We as humans are currently living between the ages of 80 – 90 on average, so even if you're 40 years old right now, then you could still potentially have a complete life left in you or more. However, this time not starting from 0, but from 40 years of experience.

The truth is that time is running out, and it's been running out since the day you were born. Today is the oldest you have ever been, but the youngest you will ever be, so why aren't you running towards your dreams as if you were on fire? Understand that it's never too late, and you can choose to change your life at any age you want. Dreams don't have an expiry date, and the only ever time that it's too late is when you're fucking dead!

<u>CHAPTER CHALLENGE</u>

This challenge is going to require that you ask yourself a series of questions which are listed below. Pull out your journal and answer these questions keeping in mind what it is that YOU really want to achieve in your life, and not what others expect from you. Take your time and don't try to rush this process. Really look deep within and be totally honest with yourself.

- **What does success mean to me?**
- **How will I know when I am successful?**
- **How will I feel physically, mentally, and spiritually?**
- **What am I willing to give up in order to achieve it?**

As we grow up, we get taught the universal meaning of success which usually looks like cars, homes, and digits in the bank, but believe me when I say that success has nothing to do with the materialistic S-H-I-T society says makes you so, and it usually has absolutely nothing to do with how smart you are. Know that success is subjective because what the word success means to me will be different for what it means to you and vice versa. You need to discover, understand, and confirm what the word success means to you and you alone. Don't ever let somebody else define the meaning of success for you. Focus on that mental image within your mind of what success looks like to you, and then visualise and feel that success every single day as you take action steps towards achieving it. Get very clear on exactly what it is that you need to let go of, give up, and stop doing in order to achieve your own version of success, realising that you can create a life that's either temporary pain but then permanent pleasure, or temporary pleasure but then permanent pain, and the choice is completely yours!

"You have to
let go of the good
to be able to
grab a hold
of the great."

MONEY MINDSET

Growing up as a child, I never had the newest toys or the fanciest clothes, and quite often I'd be dressed in hand-me-downs from my older brother or cousins. If there was something that I really wanted, then I had to fucking work for it. With four children to provide for, things were sometimes tough for my family as dad would be constantly working his ass off to keep a roof over our heads, whilst mum would make sure all kids were fed, washed, and dressed ready to then be taken to school. My parents would do anything and everything to make sure us kids had everything we needed, but when it came to the things we wanted, we would hear things like, "Money doesn't grow on trees," which is totally understandable now that I look back from a more mature set of eyes, because four children wanting the newest toys or gadgets does not come cheap!

Without even realising it, I had taken that scarcity mindset around money through to my adult life where I would be focusing on penny pinching everywhere that I could, and any money I did make, I would hoard it and do everything I could not to let it go. I'm sure you may have also heard things from your parents and the people around you like, "We can't afford that", "We will never be rich," or, "Money is the root of all evil," which are some of the most common ones. Although times may have been tough for many families, it doesn't mean that there isn't an abundance of wealth out there waiting to be discovered. It's down to you to decide that you're going to figure out a way of providing enough value to then receive riches as a result. Removing and replacing fear and limiting beliefs around money can be a transformative process that requires self-awareness, patience, and consistent effort. Remember that these beliefs have been embedded in your brain from a very young age, so removing and replacing them isn't an overnight thing.

BELOW ARE SOME STEPS YOU CAN TAKE TO DEVELOP A HEALTHIER RELATIONSHIP WITH MONEY:

1. **Identify limiting beliefs**: Begin by becoming aware of the specific beliefs you hold about money that are limiting you. These beliefs might include thoughts like, "I'll never have enough money," "Money is evil," or "I don't deserve wealth." Write these beliefs down so you can clearly see and start understanding them.

2. **Question your beliefs**: Challenge these beliefs by asking yourself if there is concrete evidence to support them, or if they are based on your past experiences that may not apply to your current situation. Often these outdated beliefs from childhood may no longer be relevant or accurate to your life now.

3. **Find evidence to the opposite**: Look for evidence that contradicts these limiting beliefs, and seek out stories of people who grew up with financial struggles but managed to overcome them to achieve financial success.

4. **Cultivate gratitude**: Focus on what you do have rather than what you lack, because gratitude can help rewire your brain to focus on abundance rather than scarcity. Regularly remind yourself of the things you are grateful for, no matter how small they may seem.

5. **Educate yourself about money**: Fear stems from a lack of understanding, so educate yourself about

personal finance, investing, and money management. The more knowledge you have, the more empowered and confident you'll feel about handling money.

6. **Set realistic financial goals**: Create specific achievable financial goals for yourself. Break them down into smaller steps and celebrate your progress along the way. Achieving these milestones will help boost your confidence and help you see that you are capable of managing money effectively.

7. **Practice positive affirmations**: Affirmations are positive statements that can help rewire your subconscious mind. Repeat affirmations related to money, such as, "I am worthy of financial abundance," or "I am working hard each day to attract wealth and prosperity," regularly to reinforce positive beliefs.

8. **Surround yourself with positive influences**: Avoid people who reinforce negative beliefs about money or who have unhealthy financial habits. Instead, seek out friends, mentors, or financial advisors who have a healthy and abundant mindset around money.

9. **Visualize success**: Take time each day to visualize yourself achieving your financial goals. Imagine the feeling of financial security and abundance, because visualization can help you create a more positive and confident mindset.

10. **Be patient and kind to yourself**: Changing deep-seated beliefs takes time and effort. Be patient with yourself throughout this process, and don't be too hard on yourself if you have setbacks. Celebrate your progress and keep moving forward.

We are living in a world where we're constantly being bombarded with ads, forever being brainwashed into believing that we lack so much, and always told that we need so much 'stuff' in order to be happy. It's so convincing, that certain individuals have actually attached their success and self-worth to the materialistic S-H-I-T like a brand-new car on finance, or the badges which are stitched to their clothing. Measuring success by the materialistic things you own, or by the numbers in your bank account will only end in misery, because it gets to a point in your life where the things you own end up owning you. You become trapped on the treadmill of life running after money, because the more money you do get, the more you upgrade your lifestyle. You buy yourself a bigger home, a better car, a newer phone, more expensive clothes, and go on even more extravagant holidays. The list goes on and never ends. Now you must put in more and more work to meet the new demands that you've personally created for your upgraded lifestyle.

Realise that you are not your home, you are not your car, your job, or the clothes you wear, and you are certainly not the number of digits showing in your bank account. If you're going through life paper-chasing then you'll be running forever. Ultimately, money is numbers and numbers go on forever, and you may begin to believe that too much money would never be enough. Of course, we all need money to live, and money is necessary to live a great life. But if you are using your money to buy the S-H-I-T society suggests, then you'll find yourself working your ass off for the rest of your life whilst running a never-ending race. Whatever you do, don't go broke trying to impress others.

Stop focusing on income and start focusing on impact and outcome. Sure, money can be used to help magnify the mission, but you should always prioritise the mission over the money. If you do this for long enough from a place of integrity where you are working towards positively impacting the lives of others, then you will end up being paid as a by-product based on the amount of value you provide to the world. Make money the result of what you do and not the reason why you do it. With money you might be able to buy things, but you will never be able to buy fulfilment, and true happiness is a byproduct of fulfilment. So, stop chasing cheques and always focus on the greater mission rather than the money. Because money will always return, but time sadly won't.

STOP WASTING YOUR MONEY ON S-H-I-T!

Many people want to quit their job, start a business, or to travel the world for instance but their spending habits remain the same. These individuals are usually 'living for the weekends' where they go week to week and from pay-check to pay-check. They have no care in the world of how much money they spend getting fucked out of their faces but are usually the first to complain about how the world owes them a fucking living, and they are also the ones who are often jealous of the people who are actually doing well in life. Remember, you can't have and become what you want by constantly repeating the same actions. Nobody became healthy by constantly eating crap, just like you can't save or invest money if you keep going out and prioritising things like drink, drugs, pubs, and clubs. Realise that your desire to change must be greater than your desire to stay the same, and never trade what you want most for what you want in the moment. Remember exactly what it is that you really want to achieve in life, and then say no to everything that isn't helping you move closer towards that.

In the western world especially, people are pressurised to pursue pay checks, in return causing them to either lose focus of what it is that they really want, or to believe that the real meaning of life is only about making money. Shifting your focus from solely chasing money to creating a life of fulfilment requires a change in mindset and approach, but also requires you to be patient with yourself as you are making the change. This is because these materialistic beliefs have been deeply engrained within your mind by society and your surroundings for many years, so understand that transitioning from a money-focused mindset to a more purpose-driven one is a gradual process.

BELOW ARE SOME STEPS TO HELP YOU MAKE THAT SHIFT:
1. **Reflect on your values and passions:** Take some time to reflect on what truly matters to you in life. Identify your core values and passions and consider how you can align your goals and actions with these values. This will give you a sense of purpose beyond money.
2. **Define your vision:** Envision the life you want to create for yourself. What do you want to achieve? And what kind of impact do you want to make? Having a clear vision will help you stay motivated and focused on your true desires, rather than being blinded by the bills.
3. **Set meaningful goals:** Instead of focusing solely on financial goals, set more meaningful goals that

cover different areas of your life, such as personal growth, relationships, health, and fulfilment, and make sure these goals align with your overall life vision.

4. **Pursue your passions:** Find ways to incorporate your passions and interests into your daily life. Whether it's through hobbies, side projects, or career choices, because doing what you love will bring you more fulfilment and satisfaction.

5. **Cultivate gratitude:** Shift your focus from what you lack to what you already have. Practicing gratitude can help you appreciate the non-monetary aspects of your life and bring more contentment.

6. **Seek a balanced life:** Balance is key to a fulfilling life. Allocate time for work, relationships, personal growth, and relaxation. Avoid letting work or financial pursuits dominate every part of your life.

7. **Surround yourself with like-minded people**: Connect with individuals who share similar values and aspirations, because being around people who prioritise personal growth and fulfilment can reinforce your commitment to creating a more meaningful life.

8. **Learn to manage finances wisely**: While it's essential to shift your focus away from just money, managing your finances responsibly will provide stability and peace of mind. Budgeting and saving can help you feel more in control of your financial situation.

CHAPTER CHALLENGE

Now it's time to really look where your money is going, because what gets measured can be adjusted and improved. Get a printout of your last 3 monthly bank statements, and then find yourself 2 different coloured highlighter pens. Take a note of the meaning for each colour. One will be for your 'WANTS' and the other for your 'NEEDS'. Look over each of the three statements multiple times and mentally scan what you've spent your money on. Then go back over them whilst specifically highlighting each of your different 'WANTS' and 'NEEDS'. Once you've highlighted everything for the past three months, then compare each month to see what your repeated outgoings look like for both your 'WANTS' and your 'NEEDS'.

Make a list of all your monthly 'NEEDS' and add up the total for one month's worth of payments that you know must come out in order for you to live and survive. For instance, this could be automatic payments or direct debits for your accommodation, travel costs, and food.

Then make a list of how much you've spent for each of the three months on 'WANTS'. Once you've done this then honestly ask yourself if each of the purchases you made in your 'WANTS' column had any benefit to your life or helped you move closer to your goal?

Now it's down to you to make the decision to adjust any negative spending habits. Don't think for one monument that I'm suggesting that all your 'WANTS' are bad, or that you shouldn't ever treat/reward yourself. But be conscious about spending your money on harmful habits that aren't supporting you to elevate your life, and habits that aren't helping you become the very best version of yourself.

Stop trading your time for money working in a job which is sucking the life out of your soul. Look, I totally understand that we all need money to survive, but why not reduce your outgoings, buy back your priceless time, and start creating the life of your dreams? Of course, choosing to chase your dreams doesn't guarantee success, but deciding to stay stuck somewhere you don't belong will only result in one certain outcome, which is eternal discomfort and unhappiness. So whatever you do, NEVER let your wage be your cage!

"I see a world where people stop chasing money, start pursuing purpose, and focus on fulfilment."

TAKE THE LEAP

Before I quit my one and only fulltime day job, I found that I was wasting my money going to pubs and clubs just so that I could spend time with other people, and the crazy thing is that I don't even enjoy drinking, plus the majority of the people I would meet up with were heading in a completely different direction to me in life. I had to make the decision to sacrifice the pubs and the parties so I could then focus on investing my money into myself and into my future. This was in the way of mentors, coaches, courses, and books. Realise that the best investment you'll ever make is to invest in yourself, because the return on investment is limitless.

I later made the decision to go against the grain by putting off potentially ever having another mortgage and moving back in with my parents, all to be able to quit my job and start creating the life of my dreams. In society's eyes this was seen as crazy and I had so many people saying, "You should wait until your side hustle covers your current wage, or even double what your wage is right now," but I personally didn't agree with that and see it from a completely different point of view. If you're in a job earning an average monthly wage, then you only have so much time to create the life of which you dream and desire. For example, I would wake up most mornings around 5 am, go for a walk, get showered and dressed, eat breakfast, brush my teeth, then leave for work no later than 7:30 am. I'd get to work for 8, and then on my breaks I would put out content online. I finished work at 5:30 pm, arrived at the gym around 6 and train for an hour, but by the time I was home and had dinner it was usually anywhere from 8 –

8:30. I would be out of the shower for 9, then I had between 1 – 2 hours to work on myself before I went back to bed.

When you're working in a full-time job, it's that much more difficult to learn something new and to spend time working on your dreams. Look, it's not impossible to create something within the free time you do have, but you are that much more restricted because many employees' day-to-day lives look the same, and that's why some call it a trap, or to be stuck in the rat-race. It's necessary to utilise your time as efficiently as possible but there is only so much you can do, and you would be extremely lucky to have a handful of hours to yourself per day whilst trying to juggle the demands of daily life. I personally felt that if I was waiting for my 'side hustle' to replace my wage then I would have been unhappily waiting forever. Sometimes in life you have to take the risk, or you'll end up losing the opportunity, because risk is the price you'll pay for the opportunity. Of course, it's going to be scary and uncomfortable, but never trade future fulfilment for current comfort. I knew that I wanted to evolve into somebody completely different after discovering my purpose, and that meant taking massive action to begin becoming that new and improved version of me. I realised that the way I could do this was to buy back my precious priceless time by building up a pot of money, and to then sacrifice the comfort and safety net of a monthly wage.

I believe that if you really want to leave your job to find out what you truly want in life, and to begin building the life of your dreams, then one of the best ways to do this is to buy yourself a window of time in which you can start discovering and designing the required action steps you need to take in order to make your dream become a reality.

This could involve saving up 6 – 12 months of money that could comfortably cover your expenses so you then could take time off work unpaid, or to even quit your job and then solely focus on you and your dreams. Obviously, the time period and amount of money is specific to each individual, so you need to ask yourself how much of both you think you'll need, and then make yourself a plan of action for what you need to do to meet your personal requirements.

I'm not suggesting you go in to work on Monday morning and quit your job with no plan of action, no support system, and no funds. But what I'm hoping to explain is how challenging it can be to find the time to work on yourself and your dreams. For many years my life looked like work, gym, home, cook, sleep, repeat, and although I didn't have dreams or a purpose back then, if I did, I would have been extremely tired from all the other S-H-I-T that consumed the majority of my time and energy. In society's eyes I had a 'good job' that paid well and was secure, but it gave me no sense of meaning, purpose, or fulfilment. So never let 'good enough' be good enough, and please realise that job security is an illusion. In some ways, Covid proved that possibly the safest job you could ever have is to work for yourself; this is because you decide your own amount of applied effort which will ultimately determine your income.

As soon as I began putting out content back in 2020 and started helping others through my own lived life experience, I knew deep down that I had found my purpose and my life's calling. The reason I knew this, was because I no longer wanted to waste any of my precious time doing the things that weren't that, and I couldn't wait to wake up in the mornings to start working on myself. Now I was living my life on purpose, it was that much more uncomfortable doing the things that did not align with my life's mission, because the more you discover who you truly are, the more difficult it becomes to remain who you really aren't. When you know who you are and what you were put on this planet to do, then every day you let go by, not doing what it is you were designed to do, is another day of your life lost to meaningless tasks.

Realise that opportunities are abundant, and they are everywhere, just like the oxygen in the air. When have you ever heard anyone walk outside their door in the morning and say, "I wonder if there is enough oxygen to go round between us all today?" Never! Nobody ever questions if there is enough, but why is it that many individuals believe there aren't enough opportunities to go around between everyone? It's because they aren't actively seeking and going after what it is that they truly want. Trust me when I say that opportunities aren't coming to you whilst sat slumped on the sofa. You have to get the fuck up and go and get them yourself by pushing yourself outside of your comfort zone, and by putting yourself in the places where your desired opportunities could potentially be. You must be willing to venture into the places that others won't, in order to discover the opportunities that others don't. You don't need to take every opportunity, because the ones that do present themselves may actually be distractions disguised as opportunities. So don't rush an opportunity but do take the ones that feel right. You'll know when it comes because you won't need to ask for someone else's opinion or even need to think twice. Your intuition will let you know, and your internal compass will always guide you in the right direction.

Covid lockdown for me was a blessing in disguise as it allowed me to pause, evaluate my life, and to eventually discover my purpose. Having that time to reflect allowed me to see how long I hadn't been enjoying my current reality. It made me start seeking change and future greater opportunities. Whilst locked down, I saw the pain that people were sadly suffering whilst stuck in their homes, and because of this I also noticed many mental health issues arising. The reason this stood out to me was because I had suffered from a deep depression a few years before, where I also felt as if I was trapped within my own home. However, I knew that I had already discovered the tools which helped me escape that prison, so decided to start sharing them with others online. I became vulnerable by sharing my own experience, and then later went on to creating and hosting a weekly mental health zoom gathering, so others could share their current challenges. This made me feel so good inside and I soon realised that my purpose was to use the knowledge I had gained from facing and overcoming the adversities in my life to help others become the very best versions of themselves.

Once I realised that I wasn't enjoying my job and was actually heading towards a dreaded destination rather than a desired one, I decided to sacrifice all unnecessary spending habits and then worked as much overtime as I possibly could. I made the decision to move back in with my parents to build up my pot over the next couple of years. This 'protection pot' allowed me to feel a little more comfortable about actually quitting my job which I had been putting off for many years prior. I was working on myself as much as I could every single day, but I only had a very limited amount of time as I was working 6-day weeks whilst also trying to juggle all the day-to-day demands of life. I remember one day I asked my boss to drop down to a 4-day-working week but he rejected my request, and this confirmed to me that if I didn't take drastic action at some point soon then I would be trapped forever.

Whilst sharing my experiences and networking with many individuals online over many months, I had some fantastic feedback and one guy wanted to jump on a zoom call with me. He asked me to reshare my story and then told me how powerful my journey was. He asked what I was now going to do with my life. I told him I wanted to quit my job and travel the world, and he instantly replied with, "THAT IS SO SELFISH!" I was absolutely gobsmacked and could not understand why he would say that. Then he explained himself. He told me it's because there were so many individuals around the world who were on the brink of suicide waiting to hear my words. Wow. That hit me hard, and I had to agree knowing full-well that I had the information others were seeking to guide them up and out of the ditches they were stuck in. Once again, he asked me what I was going to do with my life, so I told him I would quit my job and share my story all around the world. Then he replied with, "WHEN?" and I told him I don't know. He said if I didn't have an exact date then I would put it off forever and never make the decision to start this important journey. So, he asked me again and I said that I still didn't know. He said to me, "The 26th of February." To me this date meant absolutely nothing, but he said, "You'll quit your job on the 26th of February." I looked down at my laptop and saw that the 26th was the very next week! He stared through the laptop at me and said, "So are you committed?" and I sat in absolute silence, so he asked me again. "Are you committed?" My body and brain were shouting "NO!" but my gut and heart were screaming

"YES!" So, I stared back through the webcam into his eyes and said, "Yes I am committed," and he replied with, "Brilliant, let's check in with each other next Friday." After the call ended, I sat shivering with what felt like a million emotions running around my body, and the first thought that came to mind was, "WHAT THE FUCK HAVE I JUST DONE!" I was absolutely petrified and ended up spending the next week avoiding him completely.

I was terrified to tell anybody about what I was planning to do, so I kept it all to myself. However, the day before the deadline, I decided to break the news to my parents. When I got home that Thursday evening and walked through the front door, I must have had fear written all over my face. This is because when I went into the living room and sat down, my mum with her maternal instincts instantly said to me, "What's happened?" She could tell something was wrong, and I said that I wanted to tell them both something. My mum was ready to listen, but dad was more interested in watching his favourite team play football on the tv. In my mind I was hoping and praying that my dad would pay attention to the big news I was about to announce, but he clearly wasn't interested. My mum told him to listen, so he half did and then I nervously said, "I'm going to go into work tomorrow and quit my job," but before I'd even thought about taking my next breath, my dad shot up from the sofa and shouted, "Well stop fucking talking about it and just fucking do it!" Wow, that hit me hard. I couldn't believe my dad would say this to me, and I instantly felt like complete S-H-I-T. I took off up to my bedroom and sat there as a 28-year-old man bawling my eyes out. I honestly believed that my dad, who is my best mate, would have said things like, "Come on Ryan, you can do this," and then give me a massive cuddle and a pat on the back. All I received was what felt like verbal abuse and a big kick in the nuts.

As I sat there sobbing my mum came up and put her arm around me whilst trying to convince me how dad hadn't really meant to be so abrupt. Then dad came up and said he was sorry, and I quickly went from pain to perspective. This is because I suddenly realised that my dad was right, and that what he'd just said was the best thing he or anyone else could have said to me in that specific moment. In life there are what I call three types of A-Ts, and that's Action Thinkers, Action Talkers, and Action Takers. Since the year prior when the covid lockdowns started, all I had been doing was talking a good game, and that was the reason why my dad wasn't interested. Because all he had heard was me going on and on for a complete year with absolutely no action steps taken. Words alone are absolutely fucking worthless, and you'll never think your way to success without following those thoughts up with the required steps in the direction of your desired destination.

The following Friday had quickly come round, and I woke up that morning feeling as if it were D-day. I had many thoughts bouncing around in my brain all morning, and I didn't speak to anybody all day. In all honestly, I was still contemplating changing my mind and going back on what I had agreed to the week before. I thought I could keep that conversation to myself by pretending it never happened, deleting all social media, and then go back to living my mediocre mundane life. As the day dragged on, I was purposely avoiding asking my boss for the chat that evening. However, I finally plucked up the courage to ask him for a quick conversation before I left. I spent the rest of the day in silence before it rapidly got round to 5:30 which was the time I'd been dreading all day. As I was sat shaking like a shitting dog, my bullshitting brain was still trying to talk me out of it and was desperately trying to convince me that I still had time to back out.

Our ancient survival brain's only job is to keep us safe and alive at all times and does not give a S-H-I-T about our personal happiness or quality of life. So anytime it feels threatened or in any type of danger, it says, "FUCK YOU" and goes into survival mode where it literally wants to run the opposite direction. The thing is that our brain often confuses fear with danger. Back in the days when humans lived in caves it was necessary for them to have a naturally negativity bias brain, which meant to focus more on the negative aspects of life. The reason why it was vital for our earliest ancestors to constantly seek out negativity was because there was always the imminent threat of danger, usually in forms of an attack from something like a sabertoothed tiger, hence why it was essential for those humans to always be in a heightened state of emotions. They constantly had to be in that fight-or-flight mode just in case one day they walked out of their cave and came face to face with a predator, so for them it was actually life or death. The crazy thing is that we as civilised humans have dragged that same brain with us through to the modern age, even though nowadays there is extremely minimal danger of ever being attacked after leaving your home, especially by a man-eating mammal!

My boss came upstairs and could see I was absolutely petrified, so he sat down next to me and asked me what I wanted to talk to him about, but my mind went completely blank and not a single word came out. I was frantically trying to think of something to say but couldn't think of the 'best' or the 'right' way to explain exactly what I wanted to say, so I just said it as it is. "I'm quitting my job." And he instantly replied with, "Well done." What the fuck? I wasn't expecting that! I had created a crazy story within my mind of how things were going to go, and it turned out to be the complete opposite. I instantly felt relieved and that the huge weight had suddenly dropped straight off my shoulders. He asked what I planned to do, so I started explaining everything I had been doing online over the past year whilst working full time too, and he then told me how great it sounded and how he would also support me in any way that he could. I felt so much better and couldn't believe I had been so fearful to have the conversation with him, which in all honesty we should have had a long time before. Shortly after, I had replaced my fear with fun as we were both sat there laughing and joking about all the great times we had experienced over the many years, and then he began to tell me how he also quit his job when he was younger to go and travel the world. This made me feel even more at ease, and I went home that evening knowing full well I had made the correct decision.

At that moment in time, I believed that I needed to go on many different courses and have all these certificates in order to be able to help others, but that's really not the case. I grew up believing knowledge is power, so spent many months learning new things and was regularly researching the 'best ways' in which I could help others. Of course, it's important to constantly be improving your knowledge, and it's necessary to be a lifelong learner. However, many (me included) get caught on the 'research stage' whilst convincing ourselves that we need to complete course after course and have a bunch of certificates under our belts before we can begin to start. Realise that this is just a S-H-

I-T excuse for procrastinating, because the best certificate you'll ever have is the certificate of life from your own lived experience. The world is full of information and not enough implementation, so understand that the knowledge in your head is useless unless used, because it's applied knowledge that is the key to success.

If you want to do something that you've never done before then it's going to require you to take uncomfortable and unfamiliar action steps. If you want something you've never had then you must do something you've never done. Realise that you don't have to be great to start, but you have to start in order to be great. So, stop thinking and start doing, because with each step forwards you will gain a specific result that you can learn and grow from. If you're waiting for the 'right time' to start, then you may be waiting for the rest of your life. That's because there is no right time and you'll never be ready. Understand that NOW is the only time, so begin making moves knowing that progress is the by-product of taking action, and big thoughts backed up by big actions will always eventually result in big rewards. Your survival brain is defeated long before your body can't give any more, but the decisions you make after your brain tells you to stop will separate you from the ordinary and the extraordinary people in life. Taking the easy route will always reveal average results at max. However, taking the hard route will eventually gift you with the greatest experiences, knowledge, and opportunities you could ever imagine. Realise that you get to decide whether you do what's comfortable and easy or what's hard and necessary.

Taking the leap of faith to go all in on your dreams demands you to trust your own intuition and to trust in your own skills and abilities, but also requires you to have somewhat an amount of 'blind faith'. This is because success is never guaranteed and it's the reason many never make their dreams become their reality. Having blind faith is the belief that you don't really know how you're going to achieve your goal, but as long as you keep moving forwards, the path will be presented, and you will eventually accomplish what you set out to do. It's like living your life 'in the headlights' which is the same as driving your car down a dark windy road at night. You can't see all the way to the end of the road, and you don't know what potential obstacles are round each corner, but as long as you focus on the few feet you can see in front and keep moving forwards then you'll eventually get to where you want to go. This goes back to the importance of first setting your life's G.P.S and having a very clear end goal in mind. You don't need to have every single step of the way figured out; you must make moves knowing that if your WHY is strong enough then your HOW will eventually reveal itself.

Belief is something that will definitely help you achieve your goals much quicker, however doubt kills countless dreams on a daily basis. The moment you doubt whether you can fly you cease forever to be able to do it, because if you think you can or think you can't you are usually right. Nobody just believes in themselves for the sake of believing in themselves. Belief comes from the results that are gained from taking the uncomfortable action in the first place. So, with that being said, you can't truly believe in yourself until you've taken action. The great thing about this is that you don't even need to believe in yourself in order to take the very first step. Compare it to learning how to swim. You could do all the research in the world and read as many, "How to swim" books as you want, but you're never going to truly know if you can do it until you take the first uncomfortable action step which is to jump in and give it a go. Yes, it's going to be scary and no you shouldn't do it without the correct support systems around you, but until you've jumped in, you'll never know how good you are, or know what else you need to do to become better in the future. If you want to walk on water, then you're going to have to get out of the fucking boat and dip your feet into the pool of possibilities. Just know that you need to believe in yourself before anybody else does, and once you do truly believe in yourself then nothing can or ever will stop you from achieving greatness in your life.

So many people say that they are waiting for motivation to get started. This is absolute S-H-I-T because motivation is a by-product of the results you gained from the uncomfortable action you first took, and motivation itself doesn't last. If you are waiting for some motivation to get going, then here it is... YOUR GONNA FUCKING DIE! Motivation is just a temporary feeling, but discipline is going to get you from where you currently are to where you ultimately want to be. Motivation is doing something only when you feel good and when you want to do it, and discipline is to do things regardless of how you currently feel, whether you want to do them or not. Discipline is what you do whilst no one else is watching. Just think about it, you don't need discipline to do the things that aren't good for you, but you do need it for the things that are. Self-discipline is the best form of self-love, and discipline is like a muscle that's strengthened the more you use it. For example, you don't need to use your discipline muscles to eat your favourite fast food, but you do need to work them to decide to choose a healthy meal instead.

Becoming and staying disciplined requires repeated efforts and commitment. You need to start small then gradually increase the challenges you set for yourself. Even if you stumble along the way, don't get discouraged. Get back up, dust yourself off, and continue with the renewed determination knowing that discipline is a skill which is developed with practice and commitment.

BELOW ARE SOME TIPS TO HELP YOU DEVELOP DISCIPLINE IN YOUR LIFE:

1. **Set clear goals:** Define your short-term and long-term goals, because having a clear vision of what you want to achieve will provide you with motivation and a sense of purpose.
2. **Create a routine:** Establish a daily or weekly routine that includes specific activities and timeframes for each task. Stick to this routine as much as possible, as this helps train your brain to follow a structured schedule. Consistency requires you to plan your work then work your plan.
3. **Prioritise tasks:** Identify the most important tasks and tackle them first. Prioritization helps you focus on what matters most and prevents procrastination.
4. **Break tasks down:** Large tasks can feel overwhelming, making it that much easier for you to lose focus. Break them down into much smaller and more manageable steps. Completing these smaller steps provides a sense of progress and helps keep you motivated.
5. **Set deadlines:** Assign deadlines to your tasks and projects because deadlines create a sense of urgency, and also help to prevent procrastination. Be realistic but also challenge yourself to meet your goals within a reasonable timeframe.

6. **Eliminate distractions:** Minimize Distractions and remove any temptations that can side-track you from your goals. Turn off things like notifications on your phone and close any unnecessary tabs on your computer. It's important you design your environment and create a quiet and focused workspace for yourself.
7. **Time management:** Use time management techniques like the Pomodoro technique to structure your work and break intervals by setting yourself a timer for a specific period (e.g 25 minutes) and focus solely on the task at hand during that time. Then take short 5-minute breaks between tasks to rest and reset.
8. **Develop self-control:** Strengthen your self-control by practicing delayed gratification. Avoid instant rewards or distractions that interfere with your progress and train yourself to resist temptations that may hinder your discipline.
9. **Stay accountable:** Share your goals and progress with someone you trust such as a close friend, family member, or mentor. Being accountable to someone else can help you stay disciplined and motivated. This is because you don't want to let that other person down.
10. **Practice self-care**: Taking care of yourself physically, mentally, and emotionally is crucial for maintaining discipline, so it's vital to get yourself enough sleep, to eat well, exercise regularly, and to engage in activities that help rejuvenate you. Because when you feel your best, it becomes that much easier to stay disciplined in whatever it is you do.

When is it that we as humans usually take the most action in our lives? Normally when we have a clear vision of a greater future. Just think back to the last time you went away on holiday. Did you need motivation to get things done, or did you get all your S-H-I-T together because you were so excited to go? Yeah, I'm sure some of you left your packing till the last minute, but I bet no one had to force you up and out of bed that morning or beg you to drive to the airport and get on the plane. When we can see a compelling future that's greater than our current reality, we as humans start to develop some sort of 'superhuman strength' and can usually figure out and overcome challenges which are much greater than the usual ones we face. Because when your 'why' for doing something is big enough, you're then much more likely to take the uncomfortable action steps that are required in order for the 'how' to begin to reveal itself.

<u>CHAPTER CHALLENGE</u>
This challenge requires you take even more uncomfortable action by taking the dreaded leap that you know you need to take but have been putting off. Taking the leap of faith is going to be extremely scary, but just know that it usually leads to exponential growth and opportunities.

WAYS TO HELP YOU TAKE THE LEAP OF FAITH:
1. **Identify you fears:** Pull out your journal and try to understand what's held you back from taking the leap before. Once you've written down any fears or doubts you may have, you can address each of them and then work to overcome them.
2. **Set a goal:** Define exactly what it is that you want to achieve by taking the leap of faith, because

having clarity on your goal will help you stay on track, stay focused, and stay disciplined.

3. **Gather information:** Do your research and gather all the necessary information you need. Learn from and try to connect with people who have already walked the path you want to embark on and ask them of any challenges they faced along their way.

4. **Create a plan:** Make a plan of action that breaks down each of the main steps you need to take to achieve your goal, and then chunk them down to even more manageable bitesize steps that you can frequently take.

5. **Weigh-up the risks/rewards:** Before taking any action, you will feel the fear and your survival brain will try and talk you out of it, so first ask yourself these two questions:
   - **What is the benefit of taking this action step?**
   - **What is the consequence of not taking this step?**

6. **Take the first step:** Once you have your plan in place, start taking action as soon as you possibly can. Don't overthink, just start with smaller steps to obtain a series of results that will help build the momentum to keep moving forwards.

7. **Trust yourself:** Trust your journey, trust your intuition, and don't be afraid to adjust your plan if and when it's needed. Take calculated risks and don't let your fears hold you back from achieving your goals. Have faith that you have all the skills and resources needed to be successful and that you can succeed in anything you put your mind to.

8. **Celebrate the mini milestones:** Reward yourself for each win as this is what's going to help you face and overcome any challenges you may be faced

with in the future. What's the point in working your ass off to just keep working your ass off and not rewarding yourself for your hard work?

So many let the fear of looking like a novice stop them from following their dreams, but realise that everything starts at the beginning because there is no other way. Let go of the need to look like an expert to begin with, and whatever you do, don't let your EGO stop you from starting. Nobody is fully certain when starting anything new, but believe me when I say that the magic is in the unknown and in the uncertainty, because the unfamiliar is a blank canvas of opportunity for you to explore and design the life of your dreams. Many people in life are that scared of stepping out into the unknown that they permanently put off ever potentially accomplishing their dreams and desires. But it's important to realise that nothing removes uncertainty better than experience. If you start something new and feel as if you are an 'imposter' then embrace that feeling, knowing you are in the process of levelling up your life. I believe we should actively seek places and positions where we feel so far out of our depth, but rather than using the detrimental language of identifying yourself as an 'imposter' you should replace it by saying "I am a beginner," and understand how important language and self-identity are to one's overall growth and development.

START BY REPLACING THE TRADITIONAL READY/AIM/FIRE WITH READY/FIRE/AIM:
- **Get ready by preparing yourself for whatever it is that you're about to do, but don't overprepare.**
- **Take action and pull the fucking trigger.**

- **Once you're moving, begin to navigate your life in the direction of your desired destination.**

Life is going to be painful either way, but you get to choose the type of pain you go through. You can have the temporary growing pains of pursuing your personal path of purpose, or you can have the permanent pain of regret for not going after what you really want. Understand that if you don't risk the unusual then you'll just have to settle for the ordinary, and who the fuck wants that. Yes, it's going to be uncomfortable, but the most wonderful thing about taking the leap into the unknown is that if all S-H-I-T hits the fan then you can always go back to where you first began. The only thing between where you currently are and your dreams, is the story you keep telling yourself for why you can't have it. So rather than looking at all the potential risks, try to flip your focus to see all the possible future opportunities.

Know that the word 'winning' means the path and progress of struggle and strife towards a desired outcome which has a far greater value than the pain endured throughout that specific journey. So many people want to receive the pot of gold at the end of the rainbow but aren't willing to first get drenched until the sun comes out. The thing is that if there is no rain then there is no rainbow, and with no rainbow there is no pot of gold. If you're prepared to push through the temporary pain and get soaked in S-H-I-T a few times, then the path to your riches will eventually become that much clearer. You must be willing to do the things today that others won't, in order to have tomorrow the things that others don't.

"Take the leap
and the net will
appear and if it
doesn't then you'll
soon have to learn
how to swim."

FUCK YOUR FEAR

I personally don't know anybody who doesn't feel fear, or who hasn't yet feared something throughout their life. Yes, fear can sometimes serve a purpose, especially for our ancient ancestors as you learned in previous chapters. However, the majority of many modern-day fears are made up in the minds of the specific individuals. I want to start by explaining the huge difference between fear and danger; fear is not real. It is a picture we have painted within our own minds which is usually a worst-case scenario, causing us to fear things that do not currently, and may not ever, exist. Fear is an emotional response to a perceived threat or danger, whether it's real or imagined. Realise that your fears are learned behaviours most of which have been pushed on to you by the people around you, and in return you've adopted them as your own.

I had always had a huge fear of flying, in return causing me to put off going on an aeroplane until the age of 19 years. This is because I had the fear installed into my mind as a child, and I grew up believing that planes are extremely dangerous. But where did this fear come from? I had never actually experienced air travel in order to make up my own mind and confirm this limiting belief to be true or not. My amazing mum. As a young lady she decided to see what it would be like to fly in a helicopter for the very first time, but sadly due to the extremely bad experience she had, it would also turn out to be her very last time. Unknowingly she pushed that fear on to us kids and we grew up with the fear of flying.

Many individuals have had the fears of others passed on to them and in return have had their minds contaminated by other people's pessimistic mindsets, where they now focus on the worst-case scenarios rather than the rewards of life. This is such a common thing and often, the people who push their fears on to you have also previously had their current fears pushed on to them. However, it takes someone to have the awareness to realise that those fears aren't serving them, and that they need to break the limiting cycle.

Usually, the people who are closest to us like parents and loved ones, will push their fears on to us disguised as love. For instance, when they say things like, "I don't want you to do that because I love you," or "I don't want you to go there because I love you;" of course they love you, but the truth is THEY are too scared to do certain things which you do, or things that you plan to do. Because of this they then try to stop you by reminding you of how much they love you, in hopes that you won't go through with what it is that you want to do.

This can be compared to 'crabs in a bucket'. When you go down to the beach or the seaside and you see crabs that have been caught in the bucket, there is always that one courageous crab who tries to escape. However, as soon as they get to the top and are just about to make it over the barrier to freedom, out of nowhere they are suddenly pulled back down to the comfort zone of the bucket by the other crabs, and they now start to accept that their entire reality exists only within the walls of their box after realising that they will never experience what life looks like beyond the barrier of their tall bucket. Now they begin to believe that freedom will never be possible for them, so they give up on their dreams of freedom and shortly stop trying to go after what it is that they truly want.

This is the same for you and your life. Just because someone else is scared to do something, it doesn't mean that you need to accept it to be true for you. When you step outside of the norm and break the barrier of your comfort zone, it intimidates the people who are too scared to do it themselves and they now feel threatened. This is why you may notice some people say things like, "You can't do that," or "It isn't possible," but believe me when I say that it actually means THEY can't do it, and it isn't possible for THEM. Just because it may not be possible for them, doesn't mean that it's not possible for you, so whatever you do don't let someone else's limited thinking limit your actions, which in return will limit your results, and eventually limit your fucking life. Don't ever let someone who was either too scared to go after something, or who gave up on their dreams, talk you out of pursuing and achieving yours. Don't let someone else decide, design, determine, or dictate your destiny.

BELOW ARE A FEW QUESTIONS YOU CAN ASK YOURSELF WHEN IT COMES TO THE FEARS THAT HAVE BEEN PASSIVELY PASSED ON BY OTHERS:
1. **Where did I learn this fear?**
2. **How is this fear contributing to my life?**
3. **How is this fear helping me evolve into the very best version of myself?**
4. **What is the benefit of accepting their fear as my own?**
5. **What is the consequence having this fear in my life?**

Danger on the other hand is very real and we should always listen to our intuition to help keep us out of potentially life-threatening situations. Intuition is the ability to understand or know something instinctively without the need to even think about it. Most people call it their gut feeling because when you know, you know. You have a deep feeling within, that tells you to either go ahead or to avoid certain people, places, or situations. Personally, my gut feeling has been correct about everything throughout my life, but understand that you can't rely on just your intuition alone. This is because it can be great to get you out of immediate danger and to help with things like decision making/problem solving, but sometimes it can also be unreliable so it's very important to not only listen to your gut feeling, but to also ask your brain for its opinion and then back it up with the necessary and required evidence.

Realise that it's also possible to experience fear without any actual danger present. For instance, you may create a mental movie within your own mind of how dangerous doing something is, but once you've done it you then realise how it turned out to be the total opposite. However, the same is true for being in actual danger without feeling any fear. This is because some people have become that comfortable with certain situations that they have become desensitized to the feeling of fear. It's important to have a good balance between the two, because being overly fearful will prevent you from taking any risk, in return holding you back from creating and living a fantastic life, but not feeling any fear at all could potentially put you in places that could actually endanger your life.

For me, having the fear of flying prevented me from exploring and experiencing the beauty of this wonderful world which we live in for many years. This is because my anxious mindset believed that air transport was extremely risky and dangerous, and that the plane would somehow crash. But the data-backed facts are that air travel is the safest mode of transport. At that time, I was listening to my limiting belief but didn't back it up with the evidence to confirm it to be true or not.

Not only did I grow up with the fear of flying, but I also grew up with the fear of dying. However, this fear managed to stop me from facing deadly danger. After suffering through many months of mental misery whilst down and depressed after a relationship breakup, I believed that the only way out of the persistent present pain was suicide. When it got to the day that I actually planned to take my life, the overwhelming fear of death stopped me from doing something my future-self would have really regretted. This is because the fear of death significantly outweighed the desire to follow through with suicide. So in this circumstance, I managed to use my fear in my favour, and you can also do the same with your fears.

You can clearly see how fear prevented me from making the most out of life, but also protected me from taking my life. Remember your brain does not care about your happiness or quality of life, all it focuses on is to make sure you stay alive at all times. Any time you are about to do something that your brain believes to be 'risky' it will always try to talk you out of doing it. The brain is a bit of a bullshitter, plus it loves comfort and negativity. It is said that your brain has between 60 – 80,000 thoughts per day, and this is the reason why it doesn't want to work too hard. Out of these thousands of thoughts approximately 80% are negative, and 90% are repeated from the day before. Our outdated brains are naturally negativity biased which was originally to protect our ancient ancestors from definite danger back in the days where people lived in caves. So, if you don't make the conscious decision to tell your brain to fuck off from time to time, then you will find yourself stuck in that comfort zone repeating negative thought cycles until you do.

Why is the comfort zone a bad thing you may ask? Well as much as it sounds like a nice place, just realise that your comfort zone is where your dreams go to die! This is because nothing grows inside your comfort zone. When was the last time you heard someone say how something absolutely incredible and positively life changing happened to them whilst sat at home on the sofa watching a movie and eating junk food? It doesn't fucking happen, so realise that there is no growth in the comfort zone, but there is also no comfort in the growth zone. It's somewhat painful to push yourself outside of your comfort zone, but believe me when I say that in the long run the permanent pain of staying stuck somewhere you don't belong will outweigh the present pain of pushing yourself through the barrier into your next level of life.

The majority of people stay stuck in their comfort zones because their pain is bearable. Let me give you another real-life example from my own experience. Growing up as a young adult I was working as a car mechanic because I had absolutely no clue of what I wanted to do for work, and I had no help or guidance from anybody around me. For many years, deep down inside of me, my intuition was telling me I was on the wrong track, and because I was getting paid each month which allowed me to do the majority of things I wanted to do, I could put up with the pain as it was tolerable. Even though I told myself I would quit my job every new year that went by, I did nothing about it because I unknowingly enjoyed the comfort, and the pain wasn't yet unbearable. Fast-forwards a decade after I went through the depression when I re-evaluated my life and started working on myself, I realised that the pain of staying in that comfort zone of a career was so much worse than the pain of taking the leap of faith, so I felt the need to now take massive action.

For years I had all the warning signals saying, "Ryan it's time to move on," but I chose to ignore them. You, me, and many do it on daily basis; ignoring those red flags may seem ok in the moment, but trust me when I say that they will come back to bite you in the ass in the future. It all starts by getting those warning signs, just like being tickled with a feather. This is the pain saying, "Hey it's me, I'm here and just letting you know that you should think about changing something," but because it doesn't hurt yet we just ignore it. Then a little later we start feeling the pain, like as if someone was puncing you in the arm and saying, "HEY! I'm still here but you're ignoring me. Why haven't you done anything about this yet?" And again, we quite often choose to ignore that warning sign too, and that's because although you feel the pain, it doesn't hurt that much to the point where you need to do something to change it. But then it gets to the point where you have absolutely no choice at all. BOOM! It's as if a 10-ton truck has come out of nowhere and run you over. You feel like you've been broken into a million pieces and have no option other than to take action right now, and that's the pain saying, "HERE I AM FUCKER, I TOLD YOU TO LISTEN TO ME!" But now you're acting from a place of pain, fear, and desperation. You start saying to yourself things like, "I never saw this coming," and "Why didn't I listen to myself and take action sooner?" But now you don't have a choice because the universe has taken over and made the decision for you. All you can do in this moment is to hold on tight and hope for the best.

But when is it that people really start to change their lives? Usually when it gets to breaking point and they have no other option but to change. The majority aren't moved to make better life choices until it's a matter of their mortality. They have to wait until that huge fucking truck comes crashing in and wipes out them and everything around them.

Listen to me when I say that you don't have to wait for disaster to strike in order to decide, design, and deploy the next steps in the direction of your desired destination. As soon as you notice those little red flags in any area of your life, then you best act on them now to avoid that agonising appointment with the almighty universe in the future. Understand that ignoring those 'red flags' because it feels good right now will only result in long-term devastation, because once you realise the damage that's been done, then you're suddenly making doubtful decisions from a place of desperation.

You might be in a place in your life right now where the pain isn't yet quite enough to take action, and you're coming up with all the excuses under the sun as to why you can't take the first step, or for why you should just stay put. If you don't make the decision to take the first step and to start creating the life of your dreams, then you'll be forever uncomfortably comfortable, living a life of quiet desperation. Because in life you'll either make time for your dreams or sacrifice your time helping someone else make theirs. Understand that nobody is coming to save you, and nobody is coming to free you from the comfortable cage you're currently trapped in. It's down to you and you alone, to decide to break free and to begin building the life that you want and need. So, start by realising that there has never been a better day to start than today, because you will never have another day than today. Today's tomorrow will be yesterday's today. All we ever have is this very moment in time and choices to make. You need to stop waiting to start as 'right now' is the only guaranteed moment in your life, and the reality is that you will never have this moment again. So make it fucking count!

Think big but start small. Start uncomfortable and start unsure, but whatever you do start now because there is no 'perfect time' to start, and you will never be ready. If you don't take the first step now, you'll just think about it for the rest of your life. If you don't start today then what the fuck's going to make you think you'll start tomorrow? So many people are wishing for a better life, but a wish without the required action needed to make that wish become a reality will always stay a wish, so stop wishing for your dream life and start working for it, because the law of attraction does not work without the law of action. Take the first step; action creates more action, just as inaction creates more inaction, and unsure action is always better than perfect procrastination. Of course, it will be scary, but the moment you realise the pain of staying the same exceeds the pain of change, is the exact moment your actions will overcome your anxieties.

Before doing anything new or unfamiliar it can be very scary to even start due to your anxiety taking over. Your anxious thoughts come from overthinking the things in the future, and from fearing the unknown. Your lying brain starts to make up many false scenarios which can absolutely paralyse you and hold you back from becoming the person who you want to be. But don't worry because I'm going to share a crazy scientifically proven tool with you to help you overcome your anxiety.

Whenever you get really anxious about something that's coming up in your life, what happens to your body and mind? Your heart starts to beat really fast, the cortisol, which is the stress hormone within your brain raises, and your body starts to prepare for something which it doesn't know about. This is known as your fight-or-flight mode, and this was definitely needed for our ancient ancestors back in those dangerous days. But this is the crazy part. Whenever you get extremely excited about something, the exact same things happen to both your body and brain. So, when scientists measure your body and brain when you're anxious *or* excited, on paper the results look exactly the same. With this being said, it is actually possible to trick your mind to think that you are excited rather than anxious, and the way that you can do this is to repeat the words to yourself, "I am excited," over and over. It sounds so easy right, and it almost sounds like it isn't going to do anything, but the scientific tests have proven that this strategy works.

Know that your feelings come from your thoughts, and you are in charge of the feelings you attach to your thoughts, which then determines the way your body reacts. The next time you feel your heart beating really fast and when you feel stressed out, use this strategy by repeatedly telling yourself within your own mind how excited you actually are instead. This is called anxiety reappraisal which changes something within your brain, and it does this by you telling your brain the feelings and the thoughts which you personally want it to have, and then those thoughts are attached to the feelings which are actually happening inside of your body in that specific moment. When you get a negative thought come in and you let that negative anxiety build within your body, it can get so blown up and carried away that it turns into something huge. But, if you change the way you're thinking and attach the right things to the situation, you can then change the way you act based on what you're telling your body you feel. Remember that you can't choose your first thought, but you can always choose your second.

Know that fear is always going to be there, but you need to learn how to not let it overpower you and hold you back. The way you can do this is to become comfortable dancing with fear. What do I mean by this you may be thinking? Well just imagine you have your arms wrapped around your biggest fear as if you were dancing. As long as you keep moving with that fear towards the place where you want to go, then it's always going to be close to you, but it's impossible for that fear to be able to consume you.

I BELIEVE FEAR HAS TWO MEANINGS:
Freeze – Evaluate – And – Reverse
Or
Focus – Evolve – And – Relax

Fear can be an awful thing that stops you from making the most out of this unique opportunity called life, and fear can come in many different ways such as the fear of failure, the fear of other peoples' opinions, and even the fear of success. This is when you need to use your fear in your favour and flip fear for fortitude, because you can use your fear as fuel to help propel and drive you towards a future of fulfilment. Just know that the people who you look up to as 'successful' and 'fearless' are not fearless at all. They still have fears and doubts like the rest of us, however, they did not let those thoughts stop them from achieving exactly what it was that they set out to accomplish in the first place. Fear can either drown us or drive us, but understand that fear is always going to be in your life no matter what, so rather than standing still and letting it take over your whole life, get comfortable dancing with it. You need to feel the fear and do whatever it is that you first intended to do.

You're never going to think your way out of your fear because the only antidote to your fear is the fear itself. You have to do the things that scare you until they don't, by actively seeking discomfort. Voluntarily heading towards pain may seem quite daunting, however, taking small and frequent steps to expose yourself to fear and discomfort on a regular basis will help build the courage that you need to withstand the pain that you once thought you could not bear. Courage is like a muscle, and it is strengthened with use. Courage is not the absence of fear, but rather the judgement that something else is more important than fear. Courage is just fear in action, because it comes from making the decision to act even when fearful, knowing that the reward on the other side of your fear will be much greater than the momentary pain you are currently faced with. Courage creates action, and action breeds confidence. This is because the more you act, the more results you'll receive, and with every result you gain a little more confidence each time, so this is why it's vital to push past pain. Winston Churchill once said, "If you're going through hell, keep going." Because if you ever find yourself in a real S-H-I-T situation, then what makes you think unpacking your bags and setting up camp there is a good idea? In life you have to go through the S-H-I-T in order to get to the shiny stuff.

Your life will expand or contract in proportion to the amount of courage you're willing to take. No one said it will be easy, but for sure you will become more comfortable the more you lean in and take more uncomfortable actions. This is because courage is the prerequisite to confidence, meaning confidence grows as courage grows. Confidence is really the trust in one's abilities to figure S-H-I-T out. Having the courage to do something doesn't mean you aren't going to feel the fear before and during the journey, but it means that you're going to continue pushing forwards in spite of it. After all, you cannot experience courage if there is no fear to overcome. So, start looking at your fears as the training grounds of courage, because fear is usually an indicator to tell you that what you're about to do is the correct thing for you to do in this present moment of your life.

Any time you feel yourself putting something off due to fear, you should ask yourself the question, "Is this feeling just a fear or is it an actual fact?" Because many put off doing things in their lives due to the made-up fears within their own minds, which in return paralyses them for days, weeks, months, years, and sometimes even their whole fucking lives. Just think, if my dad had procrastinated when those doctors said to pull the plug on my life then you wouldn't be reading these words, so please understand that procrastination is the enemy of success and it is the thief of time, but it's only action that destroys procrastination. I'm hoping by now you understand that your time is the most precious, priceless resource that you'll ever own, so please don't waste it *thinking* about doing something. Because thoughts are just thoughts, and they are utterly useless unimplemented. You must take action on your thoughts, even if you're scared and confused, because if you believe in the quote 'time is money' then doing nothing is clearly a very expensive hobby.

YOU NEED TO A-R-M YOURSELF:
Action – Results – Motivation

Then once you've done this enough times, it will eventually build MOMENTUM and turn into a habit cycle where you feel more at ease to take even more uncomfortable action.

Stop waiting for success to come to you and start stepping towards your own unique version of success. So many are saying to themselves things like, "I'll start when…" and they think that when a certain day comes, or when this imaginary event happens that they will suddenly begin building the life of their dreams. Let me tell you that the day you are so desperately waiting to come is not coming, so stop thinking and start doing. Stop saying, "One day I'll follow my dreams" because that one day may never come. Replace, "One day…" with "Day one…" and go for it. Stop saving specific things for special occasions because this very moment is the special occasion, it's the only occasion!

You need to take the risk from time to time because if you don't risk anything then you risk everything, and the biggest risk you'll ever take is to not take any. Everything we do on a daily basis has a small element of risk to it. So, you can either live in belief or die with regret. You can also live in faith, or you can live in fear, but know that both demand you to believe in something you can't actually see, and the choice is completely yours. You don't need to be scared of failure because failure is a choice, and the only time you fail in life is when you choose to give up. You don't even need to be worried about making a wrong move, because there are no wrong moves in life. Each step you take you'll get one of two results. Firstly you'll get what you want and move one step closer to where you want to be, or secondly you'll get what you don't want and also move one step closer to where you want to be, because as much as life is about finding what you *do* want to move forwards, an equally important part of life is to figure out the things you *don't* want to also move you closer to where you want to be.

In any moment of decision, the best thing you can do is the right thing, the next best thing you can do is the wrong thing, and the worst thing you can do is nothing! Doing the 'wrong' things are also right because figuring out what you don't want in life is just as important. The truth is that even the wrong thing is better than doing nothing as life is about taking action and moving forwards. When you stop moving is when you will start to seize up and see various problems arising. There is no right or wrong because life is about progressing and figuring things out along the way. So realise that the best things come when you're moving and not sat stagnant trying to think your dream life into existence.

If you approach life with the mindset of a lifelong learner then you never really fail, because with each result you'll progress, and look at every obstruction as an instruction to guide you in what to do and where to go next. Then look at every MISTake in your life as a MUSTake knowing that you had to take that step and learn that specific lesson in order to advance to the next step. There are never any 'good' or 'bad' results when you adopt a growth mindset, because you understand that there are only priceless lessons and life experiences to be gained. You must become obsessed with becoming better and you need to grow through what you go through, because the greatest of life lessons are at the centre of every perceived failure, and all lessons in life will be repeated until the specific lesson is learned. Start asking yourself if you usually start, fail, learn, and grow or if you start, fail, think, stop, and then adjust where necessary.

If you're not ready to fail then you certainly are not ready to succeed, because the mediocre man fails and gives up, however the people you see as successful voluntarily fail until they eventually succeed. In life winners never quit and quitters never win, because winners will always find a way over, under, round, or through any obstacle that they are presented with. Understand that failure is not fatal nor is failure final, but failure is feedback. Failures are the essential road signs on the road to success, and they are where all the greatest life lessons are hiding. Failure isn't the opposite to success - it's actually part of it - because failure is just success in progress, and fucking up is the first step to finding out. The people who lose in life are the ones who stop as soon as they fail, but people who win will fail until they finally succeed. The moment you stop failing is the exact moment you stop succeeding. Recognise that you don't make mistakes anymore and that you are choosing to let mistakes make you, because every experience you go through in your life presents an opportunity for you to learn what matters to you and what doesn't. Every time you think you 'fail' at something you need to start looking at it as your, "First, Attempt, In, Learning," because if you think of it like that, then do you ever really fail if you end up learning something? In life you either win or you learn, and you only have to be right once to win.

Just imagine laying there on your deathbed and your creator said to you that you can go back for one more day to do whatever you wanted. Only for another 24 hours to do what you want before it's all over. What are you going to do? Go and tell all those people how much they mean to you, and how much you love them? Go to do that thing you've always wanted to do but had been putting off? Or are you just going to sit there in the exact same position and just think about it for a year until it's too late and that opportunity has passed? No, you're going to get the fuck up and start making moves regardless of how you feel, because fear ceases to exist in the mind of a man who's on a mission, and if at any point it does show its ugly head then that fear will never stop him from achieving all that he set out to do in the first place.

When you have an overwhelming obsession to achieve anything in your life then you can't stop thinking about taking those steps closer and closer to whatever it is on a constant basis. You literally go to bed thinking about it, and then wake up in the morning bursting to jump out of bed to actually do it. As soon as you realise the reward of achieving that specific thing outweighs your current fear, then, as if by magic your fear will instantly disappear. Yes, your fear may and most likely will come back, but now you know what you need to do in order to make your dream come true. But if you don't follow through then fear will win, and sadly for you, your dreams end up in the bin.

Know that your next level of life is waiting for you at the centre of discomfort, because the only way out of your current reality is through your present pain. Stop trying to avoid that pain and start leaning into it. But what is it that's ultimately going to help you push through that pain? It's got to be worth it to you, because when something seems like it's worth it to you, you're likely to be able to push past pain, be comfortable with the opinions of others, and to keep on track no matter what S-H-I-T may come your way. Everything which is hard to get may not be worth it, but everything which is worth it is certainly going to be hard to get. Fear will supress your progress but realise that if you were brave enough to start then you are certainly brave enough to finish. The results you achieve today will be in direct proportion to the effort you apply. You will never evolve from the comfort of the familiar because your dreams don't work unless you do. Your dream life begins where your comfort zone ends. If you want your life to be more than what it already is, then you're going to have to do more than what you already do.

CHAPTER CHALLENGE

Fear is something that can either hold you back in your life and prevent you from becoming your best self, or it can be used as a tool to push you forwards and help you break through the barrier to your next level of life. This challenge is going to require you find and start facing your fears. Start by sitting somewhere quiet and pulling out your journal to begin writing down your fears. Firstly, get as many of your fears out of your head and on to paper, and secondly take your fears and list them in order, starting with the ones you fear the most first.

TAKE THE TOP THREE FEARS THEN ASK YOURSELF AND ALSO ANSWER THESE THREE QUESTIONS:
What is this fear stopping me from having in my life?
What is the benefit of overcoming this fear?
What is the first step I could take to overcome this fear?

Stop waiting for the 'perfect' moment to start because now is the perfect moment. It's the only moment. You must change your relationship with failure by replacing, "What if I fail?" with "What if I succeed!" Now it's time to take the steps towards overcoming your fears, and which order you do this in is entirely up to you. For instance, you could go straight in with overcoming your greatest fear first, which in return will then make all your other fears that much easier to face and destroy. Or if you're not feeling up to it as of yet, then you can begin building a series of smaller results which will compound to much greater results with time. The way you can achieve this is to find the easiest entry point by choosing a fear with the lowest barrier of entry. Choose the thing from your list that you fear the least and just go and do it. It will probably be uncomfortable but it's far from impossible. Turn your 'wants' into 'NEEDS' and 'MUSTS' and watch your life instantly level up!

"Fear can either prevent you achieving, or it can push you to receiving the life of your dreams."

OPINIONS ARE S-H-I-T

For over 12 years I had been working in my one and only day job, so me taking the leap of faith was looked at as crazy by the majority of people who I had around me. Fear was getting thrown at me from all angles, and I had many of those uncomfortable crabs we previously talked about trying to pull me back down into their bucket just as I approached the tipping point to freedom. The thing is, when you start making moves for yourself, it's a guarantee that you'll have so many opinions pushed your way, but believe me when I say that the majority of them are S-H-I-T and it's down to you to decide which ones are and which ones aren't.

I remember there was a time when I was desperately seeking the advice and opinions of others. I would go down the local pub and start asking people for advice on what they thought I should do with my life. Of course, I had so many different thoughts from many different people, but now looking back from a more mature set of eyes, I can honestly tell you that there was not one piece of advice I have listened to or implemented in my life. This is because I was repeatedly getting advice like, "Get yourself another mortgage," and "You need to get another girlfriend and settle down." What a load of S-H-I-T! This was all coming from the mediocre-minded man who was happy to work his ass off in a job he didn't enjoy, to then pay for society's subscription of a pre-planned lifestyle each month, and then use any of the leftover shrapnel in his pocket to drown his sorrows in his spare time over the weekends, only to then go and do it all over again starting on the following Monday morning.

Nobody knows what's best for your life more than you. Maybe right now you think you don't know, but you best believe me when I say that deep down inside you've already got all the answers you want and need. Asking someone else for the advice on what you should do with your life is pointless, and especially if you're asking people for directions who have never walked that journey themselves. It's like asking someone for a specific set of directions to a place they've never been, and these people don't even have a clue where they currently are or where they are going. So never take the advice from somebody who isn't qualified to give it to you. Don't take advice from someone who hasn't yet been to the place where you want to go, and don't take the advice from someone who you wouldn't happily trade places with. I was asking individuals who had very minimalistic village mindsets for advice on how to create a limitless life of abundance, but because they didn't know what that type of life looked like they could only advise me from their own reality. Maybe their advice worked for them, but it definitely wasn't going to work for me. Always check the source of your information or advice and realise that the worst advice you'll ever receive is the wrong advice!

I remember when I first took the leap of faith to follow my purpose. There were people around me who were triggered and started to tell me all the things that could potentially go wrong, and why I should just focus on living a, "Normal life." WHAT THE FUCK IS A NORMAL LIFE? To me living a 'normal life' means to live an unhappy, unfulfilled, and unsatisfied life of lack where you're constantly stressed out, overworked, and underpaid. It's where you are striving to survive and not thrive, and why wouldn't you aim to be, do, and have anything and everything you dream and desire in this unlimited ever-expanding universe?

Don't ever let the limited thinking of other people convince you that you should water down your dreams to make them feel comfortable, because the only limitations you'll ever have are the ones which you've created within your own mind. This is your life, so you need to do exactly what you want to do, and not what other people want or expect you to do. Be your true authentic self and stand out from the crowd, because if you don't stand out then you'll just have to fit in, and who the fuck wants to fit in? You should never dim your light just to make others feel comfortable. Always be your true fully-authentic self, shine as bright as you can, and then set this fucking world on fire with your greatness; because you are unique and that is your superpower. There is only one of you and there will never be another one of you. We are all born originals but most die copies, so always be yourself and show the world the real you, because you can't fake authenticity. It's inevitable that you will lose people when you become your true authentic self, but understand that those people didn't really love you, but they loved the fake version of you. Because when you're living a life that's true and authentic to you, you'll end up seeing a lot of fake friends and people around you disappear. That's good, because we need to go through a stage of sifting out the S-H-I-T in our lives from time to time, and by being who you truly are you'll start attracting the right kind of crowd towards you. Then you'll notice that the people who want and deserve to be in your life will start to be attracted towards you. When you're living authentically you will never feel the need for validation or confirmation from anybody but yourself. By letting these people go you didn't actually lose them, because the reality is that they actually lost you and you just gained a little bit more of your true authentic self. In life it's your job to find your true self and not to make people like you.

A lot of people will start to show their true colours the moment you stop doing what they want, and the moment that they believe you are no longer a value to their life. Don't live a life being someone you're not just to fulfil someone else's needs and desires, or to think that you're going to make someone else happy by putting on a fake personality. Always stand out from the rest and be your genuine self because you have to be different to make a difference, and you have to stay true to yourself. Your soul knows what's best for you, and it knows what you really want. Always say what you mean and mean what you say, because the people that mind don't matter, and the people that matter don't mind.

Realise that we are now living in a world where people are rewarded for being fake and hated for being real. Making the choice and having the courage to be your true authentic self in a world that is constantly trying to make you somebody else takes tremendous strength and vulnerability, but life is way too short to be anything other than your true self. So stop living this perceived perfect life through a fake 'insta' filter, because nobody really cares about the clothes you wear, the car you drive, or the home you live in, and the ones that do care aren't your people. Your type of people just want you to be yourself, so show the world the true you and you will then attract those types of people towards you. It all starts and ends with you. Realise that we are all born ourselves but most die as someone else as they let the opinions of others talk them into living a boxed in life, bound by the solid walls of society. So many people will tell you what you should do, and they will all have opinions on what you've already done, what your currently doing, and what you plan to do in the future, but just understand that opinions are like assholes because everyone has one and they all stink of S-H-I-T. Other people's opinions of you and what you do will never put money in your pocket or happiness in your heart, so listen to yourself knowing that the only opinion that matters is your own. If you don't stay true to yourself then you'll ultimately live each day in misery because suffering comes when your actions contradict your dreams and desires.

Stop looking outside for the answers that you already have inside of you which are waiting to be discovered and stop waiting for permission from others to begin building the life of your dreams. The only permission you need is your own to then decide that you're going to do whatever the fuck you want, regardless of what others think, say, or do. If you're waiting for someone else to tell you that it's ok to begin, then you could be waiting for the rest of your life. If you're going through life relying on other people to give you all the answers, then you're likely to find yourself very disappointed at some point. This is because most people can't even be relied upon or figure S-H-I-T out for themselves, so what makes you think they are going to miraculously show up, give you all the information you need, and then help you achieve all your dreams?

BELOW ARE SOME WAYS IN WHICH YOU CAN STOP RELYING ON OTHER PEOPLE'S ADVICE AND OPINIONS AND START TRUSTING YOUR OWN:
1. **Reflect on your values and priorities:** Take time to think about what really matters most to you in this specific moment of your life, and also

remember what your current goals are as this will help you make your own decisions which align with your own values and priorities, rather than the ones of others.

2. **Start small:** Start by making small decisions by yourself, for yourself, as this will help you develop your decision-making skills, and help build your self-trust, then with each result you get you'll gain more confidence to be able to make much more difficult decisions down the line.

3. **Block-out external noise:** Limit your exposure to the S-H-I-T that's going on around you like negative news, social media, and complaining people. This will help you tune into your own thoughts and feelings, which will then allow you to make better decisions which will also be much more beneficial to your progress and overall well-being.

4. **Practice self-awareness:** Pay attention to your own thoughts and feelings when decision making, as this will help you tune in to your own inner voice and will also help you connect with your own internal compass. This can then help guide you towards making the correct decision and in return can contribute towards you achieving what you really want and need in life.

5. **Embrace mistakes:** Always remember that the mistakes you make are an essential part of your learning and growth process and are necessary in order for you to then be able to learn and progress on your personal path. So don't be hard on yourself when you make a mistake, use it as an opportunity to become better and thank yourself for pushing yourself to try new things. Because if you aren't

making mistakes then you aren't trying hard enough.

Know that people are going to talk S-H-I-T about you, and it may trigger you to want to react, but just realise that this is a test to see if you're actually focused on your goals or their opinions. Know that triggers are a blessing in disguise as they are the best of all life's teachers. This is because when you feel triggered by what someone says, it is showing you exactly where you are not currently free in your life.

You need to understand that words only affect you to the degree in which you already believe them. Just imagine if someone come up to you and said, "I hate your bright green hair because it makes you look stupid!" You already know full well and are completely certain that you don't have bright green hair, so that opinion doesn't faze you in any way at all. However, when someone says to you something like, "You will never be able to do that," and you feel triggered, then it's showing you that you have self-doubt issues, and you don't yet fully believe in your own abilities. If something similar to this happens to you, then you need to thank those people as they have just shown you the exact area you need to work on in your life.

CHAPTER CHALLENGE

This challenge is going to require that you start seriously questioning the opinions of others, to stop seeking validation, and to also start listening to your own internal voice next time you're making decisions. Next time you are seeking advice or validation from somebody else, I challenge you to consciously interrupt that pattern and search for the answers internally. Take out your journal and write down a list of all the people whose opinions really matter to you, and then always question yourself before taking advice from anyone else.

If you're always worried about the opinions of others then you'll constantly be overwhelmed with choices to the point that you procrastinate and then make no decisions, which in return keeps you stuck in the same position. You're making yourself overwhelmed by over thinking and under acting. The only way past this is to start making choices knowing that no decision is a bad decision. This is because all decisions will move you one step closer to your end goal, because you either get what you do want, or you get what you don't want, and both have benefits; getting what you don't want helps you eliminate another thing from the equation to then be more likely to receive what you do want in the future.

BELOW ARE SOME QESTIONS YOU CAN ASK YOURSELF BEFORE TAKING SOMEONE ELSE'S ADVICE:
1. **Is the person giving me advice qualified or experienced in this area?**
2. **Does the person have any biases or conflicts of interest which might affect the advice they have given me?**
3. **Have I considered other points of view and perspectives around the matter?**
4. **Does the advice I've been given align with my own goals and values?**
5. **Have I first done my own research and due diligence on the subject?**

6. What are the potential risks of following this specific advice?
7. Is this advice based on sound evidence and backed by proven strategies or results?
8. Does this advice take into account my current circumstances and unique needs?
9. Is this advice realistic and achievable based on my current situation?
10. Am I comfortable with all potential outcomes supposing I follow this advice?
11. What is my body, gut, and intuition telling me about this specific piece of advice?
12. Would acting on this advice move me closer to or further away from my current goals?
13. What do I really want right now?

Caring about other people's opinions is pointless because most people don't even know what they think of themselves, so why would you let their thoughts of you and what you do worry you? Learning to trust your own judgments, instincts, and decisions can be challenging, but it's a process that must be exercised frequently as it is essential for your own personal happiness, growth, and development.

"Never make decisions based on the advice of those who haven't yet seen the results or faced the consequences of taking it themselves."

TRUST THE PROCESS DON'T RUSH THE PROCESS

We are living in an ultrafast-paced world where we have been conditioned to receive things in an instant, and when we don't, the inpatient population kicks up a huge fuss when things take 'too long'. Our brains have been trained to expect things immediately, what with things like Uber Eats and Spotify, along with Netflix and chill. Long gone are the days of going down to your local Blockbusters praying that they had the film you wanted to watch in stock, when now all you need to do is click a couple of buttons and you have access to all the movies you could ever imagine at your fingertips. Just take a moment to appreciate and think about how privileged we are to be living in times of tremendous technology that's always advancing and improving. We are lucky enough to have complete access to the whole world with the help of a small device that sits in the palm of our hands. Your smart phone has the ability to help you do, be, and have anything you could ever imagine, and inside of it you can find things all the way from your bank, bakery, and barbers to your library, laundry, and love life.

I'm sure you're wondering why I'm telling you this and how this information can be beneficial to your life. The reason is because when you're pursuing your personal path of purpose to create the life of your dreams, you can't have the same approach that we've been taught to believe is a given right. The greatest things in life are usually the most difficult to acquire, and it can be quite unusual to achieve or receive something substantial overnight, hence why many people do not stay consistent in following their dreams and give up at the first signs of struggle.

Let's compare creating your dream life to how we as humans are created. I'm sure we can all agree that it takes roughly 9 months for a human baby to be born, and that the first step to the process is usually the most exciting. Soon after the mother notices things are changing with her body, she starts to hurt in certain places and feels sick sometimes. She later finds out which gender her child will be and still enthusiastic, starts thinking of names, begins to buy clothes, and gradually tells the people closest to her about the wonderful creature she's creating. Now many months in she is extremely tired, and her back is hurting. Sometimes you'll hear her say things to herself like, "Why did I think this was a good idea?" or "I've had enough of this pain now." Other times she has thoughts going through her head questioning if she should have even started this process, and also feels as if she wants it to all be over. But then she is given a due date and can now start to see the finish line, which in return gives her that well-needed boost of energy to keep going. Now almost at the end, she is a bit stressed and overwhelmed trying to figure out if she has everything in place for when her newborn baby arrives. THE DAY HER WATERS BREAK! Now its ALL-SYSTEMS-GO and no amount of preparation could have prepared her for this. She is in absolute agony and feels as if her life is coming to an end as each hour of persistent pain passes by. Now she starts screaming things like, "Never again" at her partner as he sits patiently beside her not knowing what to do. Suddenly the midwifes start screaming, "It's time to push as hard as you possibly can," but the exhausted mother feels as if she has no energy left to do it. She is so close to giving birth to her beautiful baby, but has no fuel left in her tank to complete the labour of life and she's now crying out things like, "I can't do it," but the people who are the closest to her are all confirming to her that she can! Absolute silence, but then after a brief moment, that silence is filled with the loud cries of life as that beautiful bundle of joy takes its first big breaths. The tremendously tired mother lets out a huge sigh of relief as she realises that the strenuous slog is over, and as soon as she feels the presence of her child, all that previous pain is instantly forgotten. The people around her cheer and congratulate her for pushing past the pain as she is presented with the precious priceless prize of her hard work... which is her newborn baby. Her partner joins them in this magical moment and tears of euphoria flow from the eyes of both elated parents. As they look into the eyes of this miniature miracle the mother looks to her partner and says, "it was so worth the struggle!"

This is the same for creating the life of your dreams. When you first start out after making the solid decision that you're going to do whatever it takes to achieve your dreams, you are filled with an extreme amount of energy and excitement. You are working much harder than ever before, and it feels like you are almost invincible. You're waking up early and going to bed very late every day knowing that you're building your future, and in all honesty, it doesn't really feel like work as you enjoy it so much. You start to meet new people and find yourself in completely different surroundings both online and in person, and soon realise that the 'normal people' around you aren't speaking to you as much, or are even questioning what you're doing with your life. Now it's becoming painful to surround yourself with certain people, or to put yourself in places that do not align with your own values, mission, and vision. Some of the people who mean the most to you start calling you crazy and then tell you how you should just stay put where you currently are. Without even realising it, that starts to rub off on you, and you begin questioning yourself. You've now come to a complete halt and don't have a clue which way to turn next. You start saying things like, "I can't do this," and "I should have just listened to them and stayed exactly where I was." But there is something which is deep down inside of you saying that there is still hope and that giving up is not an option, so you decide to make an agreement with yourself to proceed despite the uncertainty.

After making this bold decision you soon realise that there are certain individuals being attracted towards you who are keen to help, and who are giving great advice from their own similar journeys. They tell you how inspiring you are and that you should never give up, and also offer their support throughout your journey. This has given you that well needed boost of energy, and you now confirm in your own mind that you were right to keep pushing forwards. Once more you are feeling unstoppable and you're now pushing forwards harder than ever before. Things have taken a turn for the better and you feel so happy that everything is unfolding exactly how you want it to. You sometimes pinch yourself and say, "This is almost too good to be true!" Maybe it is, because out of nowhere BOOM! S-H-I-T hits the fan, and it feels like your whole world has just been flipped upside-down. Then for good measure, the naysayers around you remind you of how they knew things were going to come crashing down, and how you would have been much better off to stay where you were. You have now found yourself at one of life's most important intersections and you have the choice to go forwards, go backwards, or to stay stationary.

You know deep down that you must keep pushing forwards despite this temporary challenge. However, there is a little fucker of a voice sat on your shoulder telling you how you have bitten off way more than you can chew, and how you'd be stupid to think you can achieve your dreams. This voice is tediously talking in your ear all day every day, and you can't seem to shut it up, so you end up procrastinating for a few days and do absolutely nothing. You now find yourself saying things like, "Maybe they're right" and "I don't have a clue what to do" within your own mind, but that little ember of light is still burning deep down inside of you, and it's telling you to give it just one more go. Although everything seems to be going wrong around you, there is still something that's going right inside you. It's that internal voice which is your guiding compass begging you to be brave enough to give it one more shot. Although the little S-H-I-T on your shoulder is much louder and gets in your head, the voice from within makes more sense and those words penetrate your soul. You know that those words are being spoken from your true authentic self so decide to give it one more push. You're unsure where to start but you do. You take that next step and then another one. Before you know it, you're building momentum and things are starting to be pieced back together, and now things are back on the up again. You still have the pessimistic people around you who are projecting their perceived problems regarding your plan back towards you like they have already fucking walked the path which you are currently on, but you're not bothered because you know full well that they have never embarked on a journey that's anything like the one that you're on. On the other hand, you have a small number of individuals who are still rooting for you, and they tell you how much they believe in your abilities to figure things out. You keep pushing forwards and with every unsure action step you take, you realise that the road becomes that much clearer, and then out of nowhere the person who you needed the most in this very moment enters your life and offers to guide you through the next steps as if it were a blessing from above. You thank the universe and say to yourself, "I'm so glad that I listened to my intuition," and then within a matter of months you end up going on to achieving the goal that you set out to accomplish in the first place. You are filled with a deep feeling of gratitude and fulfilment, and you thank everyone who helped you achieve you dream, even the ones who didn't believe in you. Finally, you thank yourself for not giving up, for trusting yourself, and for pushing through the most painful period of your life.

What can you learn from these two examples? The most obvious thing is that great things take time to create, but I also want to explain the difference between instant gratification and delayed gratification. We are living in a world of instant gratification where people start things and expect to see instant results almost overnight. Some examples of instant gratification can come from things like consuming drink and drugs where you take an action and get an almost instant result. I'm sure we can all agree that these instant results are not beneficial to our overall health and long-term happiness, hence why we should focus on delayed gratification. This is where you put off pleasure in the moment for a potential reward in the future which is much greater. Just know that delaying your gratification does not guarantee success, but as long as you stay focused on what it is that you want to achieve and keep making moves forwards then there is no way you can ever fail, because the only time you ever fail in life is when you choose to give up. Failure is a choice because whenever we get knocked down in life, we all get to choose whether we give up or get up. So, trade instant gratification for instant application and start taking action steps towards your dream life.

You can see how it's so important to trust the process and not to rush the process. Not for one moment did either of the parents try to speed up the birthing period, because they knew that from the day they realised they were having a baby, that they had to wait around 9 months before they would hold their baby in their arms. It's the same for you creating your dream life. Just understand that you most probably won't see many, if any results of your hard work for months, and sometimes even years down the line. Don't let this discourage you from taking action, because you need to realise that the day you plant the seed is not the day you eat its fruit. You need to delay your gratification by having the long-term vision within your mind, and to focus on the tasks and not the target. Focus on the one or two steps that are in front of you and take action steps forward that align with your vision, knowing that with every step you do take, whether it looks like a 'good' or 'bad' step, you are moving one step closer to achieving your dreams. You will quite often have to do the things you know you need to do despite not feeling ready to do them.

Whenever you embark on this journey, you'll undoubtedly find yourself face to face with a 'turnback moment'. This is when you convince yourself that things aren't working, it's too hard, you should have stayed where you were, or that you should just give up completely. When this does happen to you, you need to understand that the only difference between standard people and successful people is that the ones who achieved success in their lives came to this junction but decided to keep moving forwards despite the lack of information they had about the route ahead. They also kept pushing forwards despite seeing everyone else along the way holding up all the warning signs which were telling them all the reasons for why they shouldn't go any further, trying to remind them why they should just turn around and go back to where they once began.

A big part of trusting the path you're on is to understand and believe that everything which happens is happening FOR you and not TO you. Rather than having paranoia around the process, you need to focus on the opposite which is pronoia. Pronoia is the belief that everything which happens in your own unique world is happening in your favour. You will fuck things up, people will S-H-I-T on you, and you will get a lot of NOs along the way, but you need to realise that the momentary pain you are presented with is all happening to prepare you for what's to come. So, look at every obstruction as an instruction and every rejection as a redirection for what to do and where to go next. This is why I believe it's so important to find something you would die for and then fucking live for it. Because when you're living your life on purpose by working towards something which will help contribute to a much greater cause, you are then able to withstand the majority of things that try to knock you off track along the way. Of course, the road is long and sometimes super tiring, and a lot of the time you will feel like giving up. Stopping isn't going to get you there any quicker, and this is the reason why so many give up on themselves and on their dreams. You should never fold whilst still unfolding because there is always a breakdown before any big breakthrough. The truth is that you don't know how close you could be to achieving your dreams. Sometimes all it takes is just one more big push to break through that barrier and step into your dream life. This is why you should never give up; you didn't come this far just to get this far. As long as you've got clarity on exactly where you want to be, then with enough consistent steps repeatedly taken towards your desired destination you will eventually get there. Direction is way more important than speed, and slow progress is better than no progress.

It's also very important to be grateful for everything that comes your way, even the perceived negative things, because these things are usually what teach you the most valuable life lessons. You need to be positively dissatisfied with your life, which is being grateful for where you currently are, but excited for where you are going to be.

CHAPTER CHALLENGE

This challenge is going to require that you schedule daily and weekly check-ins with yourself to keep track of your progress towards your greater goal. Every day block out 5-10 minutes in your timetable for you to sit with pen and paper and review your action steps and progression. Then at the end of each week, take a some more time to reflect on what went well and what could have gone better, and then make any necessary adjustments going into the following week.

BELOW ARE SOME WAYS THAT CAN HELP YOU TRUST YOUR JOUNEY THAT MUCH MORE:

1. **Embrace uncertainty:** Realise that life is full of unknowns and many unexpected things can and usually will happen, but instead of worrying about the future, enjoy this uncertain moment knowing that it's normally where the greatest of opportunities are found.

2. **Focus on the present:** Instead of worrying about what might happen, focus on what is happening in this present moment. Take one step at a time and trust that with every step you take, you are moving in the correct direction. Stop thinking, "What if" and start feeling, "What is!"
3. **Let go of control:** Trying to control every single thing in your life can be extremely exhausting and very counterproductive, so learn to let go of total control and trust that the universe has a bigger plan for you, and that things will eventually work themselves out.
4. **Stay positive:** Keeping a positive perspective and outlook on life can help you trust in your journey, and also help welcome more positive things into your life. Having a positive mental attitude alone isn't going to achieve your dreams, but it's certainly going to help. If you don't believe me then try doing it with a negative approach and see how you get on.
5. **Seek support:** Surround yourself with other positive people who believe in your abilities and who can also help support you on your journey, because their encouragement alone can help you stay on track and contribute to increasing your own belief in yourself.

So many want instant gratification and aren't willing to make the necessary sacrifices, or to take the uncomfortable action which is needed in order for them to eventually achieve their dreams. They then get pissed off with the results they got from the action they didn't take. Don't get me wrong, hard work is hard, but living an unfulfilled life, not becoming your best self, and not doing what you truly want to do, is much harder in the long run.

The crazy thing about life is that all our unique paths are so dissimilarly similar. This is because although each individual journey is completely different, the final destination is always the same, which is to arrive at death's doors. I have never heard someone say, "I can't wait to get to death!" So, stop focusing on your end destination and start focusing on enjoying your present pathway. Trusting your journey is a challenging process that takes time and effort, but it is an essential piece to your puzzle of fulfilment, so be patient with yourself and keep moving forwards with a positive attitude. This somewhat scary trip is going to take time and a lot of courage, but the person who you become along the way outweighs any potential pain you may face during the journey, because the reward is always the journey itself and never the destination. Believe in yourself and all that you are, knowing that you have something deep inside of you much greater than any obstacle you may come across.

"People overestimate what they can do in a year and underestimate what they can do in a decade."

TIME IS TICKING

As much as it's super important to focus on delayed gratification, it's also very important to remember that time is passing by, and that it slows down for nobody. We all have the same 86,400 seconds to use up throughout the day, and I believe you can change your life in one single second. So that's 86,400 potential opportunities to change your life for the better. This is why it's vital to focus on the daily tasks that need to be taken in order for you to build a series of small steps, and then over time these little leaps will compound and eventually become the big results. Your life is ABSOLUTELY fucking priceless my friend, and every single second you let slip, by doing something that doesn't align with the true you, is another second of your precious limited time here on earth wasted.

Whatever happens the clocks are always going to keep turning and the earth is always going to keep spinning, so it's down to you and you alone to make the most out of every single second you've been gifted in this wonderful world. Don't take any day for granted because yours, mine, and everyone else's days aren't promised, because we're all on borrowed time. Never forget that just you being here on earth right now in this very moment, is the most magical, mind-blowing, magnificent miracle you could ever imagine. If you don't think so, then understand this. We are currently a group of around 8 billion unique living individual human beings existing on a rock that has the circumference of over 24,000 miles, that's spinning at over 1,000 miles per hour, which weighs over 5 trillion kilograms, and is floating in an ever-expanding universe that nobody truly knows the sheer size of, nor can they predict if, how, and when it will all end. It is said that you being born in the place you were born, on the exact day you were born, by the parents who actually created you, is approximately 400 trillion/1 (400,000,000,000,000 - 1). The truth is that it's basically impossible, but here you are. So surely that goes to prove that miracles do happen on a daily basis? Do not think for one moment that it's not possible for you to create the life of your dreams, and do not let the S-H-I-T that someone online has to say about you being brave enough to build your best life stop you from starting or completing your own unique journey. This is your opportunity and not theirs, and the only impossible journey is the one which was never started. So let your haters be your motivators to help drive you towards your dream life.

How many of you have ever purchased a lottery ticked with absolute certainty that you're going to win? I have, but the most I ever won was £10, but that didn't stop me from buying another the next week and trying again. As of 2021, EuroMillions says the odds of picking five numbers and the two lucky stars to win the jackpot is a 1 in 139,838,160 chance. On average we as humans are living to around 80 years old, which converts to 42,048,000 in minutes. That's 2,522,880,000 single seconds to potentially become the very best version of yourself, and to create the life of your dreams. Just imagine you had the exact same belief for designing your dream life as you did for winning the EuroMillions. Your life can completely change for the better or for the worse in one single second, and on average every human has around 2,522,880,000 (give or take) opportunities throughout their lifetime to create a fantastic future for themselves and their families through their own actions. Each morning you open the two gifts of life to see another day, you are rewarded with another potential

86,400 potential opportunities to make a change. But think of it like this, you have already won the greatest of all jackpots because we are all born winners. If you're reading these words then you have already won the most important of all competitions, because if you didn't win then you wouldn't be here on earth in this beautiful moment to celebrate your victory. So, if the odds of you being born are 400-trillion-1 then what would you say the odds are for you making the most out of your one and only unique opportunity, and creating the life of your dreams? I would say it's a 50/50 chance. You can either choose to live a life of chance, or you can commit fully and live this 'never to be seen again' extraordinary experience called life to the fullest, and the choice is completely yours.

Realise that not many things in life are 100% guaranteed, but two things are... that we are all born, and we will all die. But it's what we do with the opportunity between these two events that really matter most. We are all born with two lives but the second one begins only when you realise that you just have one, because the reality is that everyone dies but not everyone truly lives. So many are just existing, believing tomorrow is guaranteed and so they are living their lives on repeat as if it were Groundhog Day. Whilst in a coma, I wasn't conscious to decide whether to switch my life support machine off or not, and it was totally in someone else's control, and I have noticed that so many people have already unconsciously pulled the plug on their own lives. Many young adults die at 25 but aren't buried until 75. This is because they are waking up every day with absolutely no dreams, goals, or visions for a compelling and fulfilling future for themselves, in return causing them to bumble through life without a care in the world, and without any intentions for what they would like to achieve each day. Understand that death is not the greatest loss in life, but the greatest loss is what dies inside us while we live. The graveyard is one of the wealthiest places on this earth. Just imagine all of those undiscovered and unused talents, skills, and abilities that cease to exist. All of those would-haves, could-haves, and should-haves that the world never had exposure to. I personally don't want to perish filled with potential. Do you? Realise that you have greatness within you that needs to come out to be shared with the world, so never impound your importance, and whatever you do don't take your greatness to the grave!

Imagine when you were born that not only did you receive a birth certificate, but you were also given a death certificate which clearly showed your exact day of death. You could clearly see the timeline you had left to make the most out of your life with the limited time you had here. Would you do the things you're doing today knowing that your time is running out? Would you procrastinate on your dreams and let fear stop you from moving forwards?

The thing is that nobody knows when their time is up, and it could be over at any given moment. The only fear you should ever have is the fear of not being blessed with the gift of enough time in this wonderful word. The truth is that death is inevitable, and we have all been dying since they day we were born. Nobody knows when it's their time to take the treacherous trip towards the tomb, so let the reality of death be a motivator to put urgency into living your life today. The bad thing is that time flies, but the good thing is that you're the pilot. So, grab a hold of the wheel of life and start fucking steering it in the direction of your desired destination.

If I offered you £1 Million pounds, would you take it? Well of course you would, and you'd be stupid not to. But you're probably thinking what's the catch? Well, what if I said that the only condition is that you cannot wake up tomorrow, would you still take it? If like me you value your life then you won't take the money, but what if I offered you £10 Million, would you take the money but only have 24 hours to spend it all? No? Well what amount of money would you need in order to not wake up tomorrow? I'm confident in saying that you're thinking no amount of money would be sufficient enough for you to never ever wake up again, and if this is the case, then that proves your time on this earth is fucking priceless. So, realise that every day you get gifted those 24 hours you are given something that no amount of money could ever buy, and that my friends is called life!

I have another offer that may tempt you, so let me ask you this. How much would you sell just 1 year of your life for? £10k, £100k, £1M, or £10M? Knowing that it's only just one year of your life lost, you may choose to take me up on my offer. But let me ask you another question. When it comes to the very last day of your life, how much of your money would you give me to go back and live another full year? Now I'm confident in saying that you'd give every penny you had to your name. This shows that every second you let go by not doing what it is that you want is costing you, but how many years have you let fly by not chasing your dreams so far? 1, 2, 5, 10? If you're not yet pursuing your dreams, then when it gets to the end of your life you will be wishing that you could go back and use your precious, priceless time differently.

Envision this. You managed to meet your maker and they say to you, "How was your time on earth? Did you do all the things you wanted to do, go all the places you wanted to go, and say all the things you wanted to say?" and you regretfully say, "No... No I didn't." So they invite you to sit down, and on the desk in front of you are two big books. They point at the first book and say, "This is the manual I had created for your life." You pick it up and you start to flick through. You start to see pictures of your life. All of those magical maternal moments in the arms of your magnificent mother, and all of those fun times throughout childhood, teenage years, and early adulthood. But then you start to see pictures of all these amazing things, and you realise that it's all those things you were too scared to do. So, you pick up the second book and you open it up. As you flick through you see pictures of your life up till today. Sure, it's been an 'ok' life, but then suddenly you start flicking through pages of blank nothingness, and you're instantly overwhelmed with resentment, responsibility, and regret knowing full well you could never re-apply, return, and re-attempt, to re-live the life that was there for you all along. Because that's it. The journey's over, but you've only just realised it was a one-way ticket and there's no going back.

I'm telling you this because I don't want you to be in this same position when it comes to the end of your life. I want you to take what you've learned in this manual and apply it to your life so that you can create and live your dreams. Yes, it's going to be super scary, but it's going to be so worth it. Don't fear failure. Fear regret. Make the pain of regret worse than any other pain you could ever imagine. Because the pain of fear and failure is temporary. But the pain of regret will last a lifetime. Open your eyes to see that your dream life is right there in front of you ready for the taking, but you just have to reach out and grab it with both hands. So don't wait for the manual... MAKE THE MANUAL! Because hell is the possibility that when you die you meet the person that you were meant to be.

Your time is not forever so use it wisely. There is a priceless space between being born and dying which is called life, but this life really belongs to death. Because death owns this vehicle called life, and you are just leasing it. Whilst moving along this journey, you get to steer your vehicle in whatever direction you want, but be very careful with your precious time behind the wheel because nobody knows how much fuel is left in the tank, and death will decide exactly when your tank is empty. Making the most out of your one and only unique opportunity on earth, by seizing every single day to work towards building the life of your dreams is so important as life is limited, and time is always ticking. We all have an unknown amount of time to accomplish all our goals, to connect with the people around us, and to experience as much of this wonderful world as we can. Failing to make the most out of your life will most likely lead to discomfort, dissatisfaction, then eventually disappointment, and potentially disaster. However, making the most of your life has many benefits including increased happiness, improved relationships, and a deep feeling of purpose, meaning, and overall fulfilment.

Of course, there are lots of things that can prevent you from achieving your goals like fear for instance, but one of the main reasons for why you don't and perhaps won't ever achieve them is that you have nobody to keep you accountable to first take action on, and then to follow through and complete the things that you promised yourself you'll do. Know that whenever you say you're going to do something and then don't follow through with the required action steps you said you'd take, you lose a little bit of confidence within yourself and your own abilities every single time. You must finish everything you start because how you do one thing is how you do everything. If you come up short in one area of your life, then I'm confident in saying that there is most likely another area of your life where you are also not fully fulfilled. If you realise that there are things in your life which you know you started but never finished, don't be too hard on yourself, but learn to then become better. Start by looking for the reasons why you think you never completed that specific thing, then ask yourself if completing that thing is still important to you, and finally take the easiest next step to get the ball rolling again, but also don't forget to reward yourself for every little win along the way.

CHAPTER CHALLENGE

It's so important not only hold yourself accountable, but to also have someone else you can check in with to confirm that you're still on track towards achieving your goals and targets. This challenge requires you to ask a trusted companion for some support. Whether this is a friend, family member, coach, or mentor, you need to ask them to hold you accountable for starting and then following through with the goals and targets that you've set yourself.

BELOW ARE SOME WAYS IN WHICH YOU CAN HAVE SOMEONE KEEP YOU ACCOUNTABLE:
1. **Find yourself an 'Accountabilibuddy':** First reach out and find somebody who you truly trust to become your accountability buddy. Someone who won't let you off the hook or let you get away with not taking action on the things which you said you would take action on.

2. **Set clear goals and targets:** Before asking them, you need to know exactly what it is that you want to achieve or accomplish and then write this down, not only for yourself but also for the person who you trust to keep you on track.
3. **Set expectations**: Together have a clear discussion about what you need and expect from each other. This could be things like check-in times/dates, feedback, and encouragement. Tell them to be hard on you, to tell you the truth, and to not put up with any of your S-H-I-T excuses.
4. **Create a plan of action**: Work with your accountability buddy to create a plan for how you will achieve each specific goal, and make sure they hold you accountable along the journey.
5. **Celebrate your success**: Whenever you achieve certain tasks or milestones, make sure you take time to acknowledge those accomplishments, and celebrate them with your accountability partner as this will help keep you motivated and on track to much greater success in the future.
6. **Positively punish yourself:** The word punishment has such a negative connotation connected to it so please don't take this the wrong way. I'm not suggesting for one moment you do anything to negatively affect your progress, but I want you to discipline yourself for not following through with something you promised you'd do. You can do this in ways of not allowing yourself to enjoy a certain amount of free time, or to set yourself an uncomfortable challenge like going for a long run in the rain etc. The one I like the most is to tell your accountability partner that every time you slip up with something, that you agree to give them £100

of your own money (or your own equivalent) as that way you will do everything possible to avoid the potential pain of your hard-earned cash leaving your pocket.

Ultimately the importance of making the most out of life comes down to the fact that we only have one chance to do it, so by maximising every moment and then pursuing personal projects, passions, and purposes that bring us a sense of greater meaning, can leave us with fewer regrets and further feelings of accomplishment.

"You can avoid doing the things you said you would do, but you can never avoid the consequences of <u>not</u> doing the things you said you would do."

STAY IN YOUR LANE

In a world where we are constantly consumed by social media, it's so easy to get distracted and take your eyes off your goal, in return you start focusing on what others around you are doing. If you want to instantly feel S-H-I-T then I challenge you to spend 30 minutes scrolling social media, and I guarantee within a matter of minutes, without even realising it, you will start comparing your life to the perceived perfect lives of the people you see sharing photos of themselves living their best lives.

Whatever you do, don't believe all the S-H-I-T you see online because a lot of social media is fake, and believe me when I say that most people only put up their best bits. Realise that you're looking at only a small piece of their lives and these are usually the very best parts, plus you don't know what's really going on in their life. Because for all you know, those individuals you're looking at as super happy and successful could actually be so sad and stressed out trying to keep up with the demands of society. I know people who have paid a lot of money to buy designer clothes, or to eat out at fancy restaurants only so they can take a pic and post it online. Certain individuals are literally living every day for 'the gram' where they have to constantly showcase their S-H-I-T online believing it will make others think that they are truly happy and successful, when in reality they have just spent a week's wages on a night out in an extravagant restaurant, and now are feeling crap as they have no more money left for the rest of the week ahead.

Understand that we are all living our own unique lives and no two paths are the same, so never compare your path to somebody else's; it's so easy to compare your step 1 to somebody else's step 10. You need to know exactly what it is that you want to achieve in your life, and then take the daily action steps towards achieving it. You don't need to compare your journey to anyone else's, because in life losers focus on winners and winners focus on winning, so keep your eyes on your target and stay in your lane. Let other people do what they need to do to make them happy, mind your own business, and then do exactly what you need to do to make you happy. The truth is that other people don't really give a S-H-I-T about what you're doing or the mistakes you make, as they are too focused on their own lives, and the ones that do have time to criticise and hate on you don't have a fucking life, so let them carry on with it because all it's doing is holding them back from achieving greatness in their life.

BELOW ARE SOME WAYS IN WHICH YOU CAN STOP COMPARING YOURSELF TO OTHERS:
1. **Focus on your own goals and accomplishments:** Instead of comparing yourself to others, start focusing on your own progress and achievements whilst on your own journey. Set your goals and then work towards them, but not forgetting to celebrate the mini milestones along the way.
2. **Practice gratitude:** Take time each day to focus on all the things you are grateful for in your life. By doing this it can help you shift your focus from what you don't have to all the things you do have.
3. **Identify your unique qualities:** Remember that you are unique, and you have your own talents, strengths, and specialities, so focus on what it is that makes you stand out from the crowd.

4. **Limit social media consumption:** Social media can be a big source of comparison and self-doubt so consider limiting your use of social media, and to sift the S-H-I-T by clearing out the crap and unfollowing accounts that make you feel worse after consuming their content.

Living in this device-heavy age where we all have instant access to comments, likes, posts, and shares, it's become a normal thing to compare your life to someone else's, as it is almost impossible to go through a day without unconsciously comparing yourself to someone else. However, having the awareness that you're doing it is the most important thing, because when you realise that you're doing it, you can then pause the path of comparison and focus on the things that you currently have, plus the things you also want to work towards.

You have to make your own path in life because this is your life and not anybody else's, so do what makes you happy, and do exactly what you think is right. It is ok to be afraid of creating your own path, because no one said you had to be the bravest person in the world in order to create your dream life, but you do have to be willing to face your fears and go for it anyway. There will be times where you fall and you don't want to keep going, but just remember that the rewards on the journey are far greater than any stumbling blocks you may come across. Nobody who you see as super successful today saw their whole journey before they set out, but they began making moves even before they felt ready. If you can already clearly see the complete path paved out for you step by step, then I don't think it's your path. This is because you make your own unique path with every step you take moving forwards, and that's why it's your unique path. Life is about creating your own path and making the journey your own by defining what the word success means to you. The beauty of choosing to create your own path is that its unique to you, and not one which has been picked off someone else's shelf. Of course, it's important to imitate and model the success of other people's proven plans who are already where you want to be, but you will always put your unique twist on it and make it align with your own unique values. We all have a limited time on this earth and our membership could expire at any given moment, and that's why it's so important to create a life that's true to you. Why the fuck would you want to try and replicate someone else's complete pathway? Just remember that the journey of a thousand miles always starts with one single step.

CHAPTER CHALLENGE

This challenge requires you to recognise the next time you find yourself comparing your life to somebody else's, and to then halt your current comparison habit. Once you're aware that you're comparing yourself to someone else, I want you to convert your comparison into inspiration and motivation. Instead of letting comparison stress you out and make you feel S-H-I-T about yourself, you can use it as fuel to help boost you to take more action towards your goals. Instead of feeling envious of other people's accomplishments, start to think how they have already achieved what they have achieved, then start to see how you can learn from their journey. Search for ways in which you can replicate it, and then begin to implement what you learned into your own life. One of the quickest ways to success is to model others who already live the life that you want to live.

BELOW ARE SOME QUESTIONS TO ASK YOURSELF NEXT TIME YOU FIND YOURSELF COMPARING YOUR LIFE TO SOMEONE ELSE'S:

1. **How did they achieve "X" in their life and what do I need to do in order to achieve "X" in my life?**
2. **What can I learn from that person's path, and how can I use those lessons for my own personal journey?**

BONUS CHALLENGE

Next time you see someone with something you wish you had in your life, whether it's a materialistic item, a career, or a type of lifestyle they live for instance, I want you to congratulate them for how well they have done, and then if you feel it's appropriate you can ask them what they needed to do in order to achieve it. Celebrating the success of others puts out great positive energy into the universe which will be beneficial to you as it opens a pathway of reduced resistance for you to also receive the things that you want in the future.

People love to talk about themselves more than anything else, and I've personally found that by allowing somebody a space to open up about their life, and also talk about their own experiences, that they will happily share all the priceless tips and tricks that they learned along their journey. This is why it's so important to not only celebrate the success of others, but to also be interested rather than interesting. Because the more curious you are about the success of others, the more successful you will be yourself, as you will pick up on the painful lessons they had to go through on their journeys, and you can then implement those vital lessons on your own road to success and hopefully avoid those painful lessons yourself. Curiosity is always the first step to discovery.

Although comparing ourselves to others can be a natural thing to do, it can also be a source of negative emotions, and can be a breeding ground for self-doubt. So, remember to never compare other people's outsides to your insides, because the only person you should ever compare yourself to is your previous self.

"Comparison
is the thief
of joy."

FINAL THOUGHTS

I really hope you've made your way through this user manual and enjoyed the challenge of pushing yourself outside of your comfort zone, in return gaining more self-confidence, further clarity, and a set of tools that can be used to help build the life of your dreams.

Now it's your time to embark on a life-long journey of self-discovery. It will be extremely painful at certain points. However, nothing is as painful as laying on your deathbed wishing you could go back to live the life that had been created for you. Only when you find the bravery to honour the life you were put on this earth to design for yourself will you find true happiness, meaning, purpose, and fulfilment. Once this is accomplished, you will then live life knowing that you did every single thing you wanted to do up until your dreaded day of demise. The fact is that we are all going to die one day, and nobody knows when that day will be, so why not make the very most out of this unique opportunity you've been blessed with?

You don't have to wait for disaster to strike to start becoming your best self, and you don't have to wait for a tragedy to then change your trajectory. Just realise that playing it safe does not serve you, your life, or humanity, in any way, shape, or form. Playing it safe is robbing you of experiencing the full beauty of this one-time only opportunity, because the safe bet is fleecing you from feeling the real adventure that this beautiful life has to offer, and then depriving you of getting what you really want. Know that if you play small you stay small, because if you play this game of life wrapped up in fear from inside the tall walls of your comfort zone, then you stand no chance of getting what you truly want. You need to ask yourself how you want to be remembered and then do everything you possibly can to start creating a life that your future-self would be proud of. When you build a life that you love, you also inspire others to do the same, and also, many future generations to come.

If you are still yet to take your desired action steps, then I want to remind you of some of the things you must do in order to fulfil your dreams and desires. I want to start by reminding you that your desire to change must be greater than your desire to stay the same. First you need to understand and identify what it is that you want to achieve or have in your life, and then you need to figure out what has stopped you from having it already. Also look at what it is that is still preventing you from having it now. It could be fear or self-doubt for instance.

Take out your journal and write on one side of the page "WHAT DO I WANT?" and then on the other side write "WHAT IS STOPPING ME FROM HAVING IT?"

If it's a fear for instance, you could ask yourself is this fear a fact or is it false, and by having this fear how is it helping me or preventing me from achieving what I really want?

Next ask yourself the question "What is the first, easiest, step I can take to get me going in the direction of my desired destination?"

Answer both questions of, "What is the benefit of taking this next action step?" and also, "What is the consequence of not taking this next action step?"

Then put a pen to paper and write down all the pros and cons for each scenario by answering both questions: "What is the benefit of taking this next action step?" and also, "What is the consequence of not taking this next action step?" Because when you put pen to paper, you create a connection between your thoughts and what it is that your soul is really craving. Don't rush, don't overthink, let the pen do the work and get it all out of your mind and on to paper. Realise that nothing is silly or stupid as this is what's going to help you eventually get what you really want.

Realise that the price of inaction is far greater than the price of making a mistake, because if you never try then there is only ever one guaranteed outcome, which is to remain the same. So many are afraid to try and fail that they then fail to ever try, but in the end it's the things we never attempted which will haunt us for the rest of our days. This is because it's usually our inactions we regret rather than the actions we took, so realise that regret is something you will take to the tomb. Sure it's 'risky' to go after what you want in life, but risk is the price you'll pay for opportunity, and if you don't risk anything, then you risk everything. We literally only have one chance at this opportunity called life, so you can either give it all you got, or you can go with all you got. Action destroys procrastination because you can't ever think your way past the action steps you need to take in order to discover, pursue, and accomplish your dreams. Don't get so caught up on knowing every single step of the way, because all you need to do is start taking the steps towards your dream life, and when you do the path becomes that much clearer. The only thing between you and your dreams are the specific action steps required to get there.

Whatever you do, make sure you appreciate, congratulate, and reward yourself for every single step you take towards your goals, and never put yourself down for not making as big moves as you would like, because we are all our own biggest critics. Know that the steps you think are small are looked at as huge leaps by others. Remember that direction is way more important than speed, and slow progress is better than no progress. Right now, you might not be where you want to be, but thank fuck you aren't still where you used to be.

BELOW ARE SOME STRATEGIES TO HELP PREVENT YOU BEING SO HARD ON YOURSELF:

1. **Practice self-compassion:** Always be kind to yourself no matter what, and always treat yourself with the same support and understanding that you would offer to a best friend who is on a similar journey and struggling.

2. **Focus on your accomplishments:** Instead of dwelling on your mistakes or perceived failures, take some time to reflect on your success so far and all the progress you have already made.

3. **Challenge negative self-talk:** Whenever you hear that inner voice talking S-H-I-T towards you, try to replace those negative disempowering thoughts with more positive and empowering ones.

4. **Set realistic goals:** It's great to have huge goals, but always remember to have the smaller more achievable goals which will then compound on top of each other and overtime those series of small results will add to your overall belief in yourself and your abilities. In return, this will help energise you and give you the power to go on and achieve greater things in the future.

5. **Take breaks and practice self-care:** It's so important to take care of your health and wellbeing whilst on this journey, because if you don't have your health then you don't have anything. You need to look after yourself not only physically, but also mentally and emotionally by getting enough rest, exercise, fresh air, and also to engage in energy producing activities that bring you a feeling of joy and relaxation.

Remember that you are only human and as humans we all make mistakes, plus we can only get so much done in a day. This is why it's so important to prioritise the things that mean the most to you throughout each day, including yourself! Realise that the greatest of things take time to create. Rome wasn't built in a day. However, they worked on it every day. Focus on taking daily steps towards your dreams, and before you know it you will wake up one day and you will be living them. Know that anyone can become anything, but not everyone can become everything, so FOCUS on the main thing that you want to achieve in your life by 'Following One Course Until Successful'. This doesn't mean that you need to stay on a path that you're unsure is for you, but if there is something you know you really want to achieve, then start taking the consistent daily actions towards that thing until you do eventually achieve your desired result.

<u>THE FINAL CHALLENGE</u>
This last challenge requires you to write a letter of encouragement talking from the perspective of your future-self. This is your best-self looking back at your current-self, whilst watching and monitoring each and every move you take, but also supporting and guiding you through the

difficult times you find yourself faced with. This future best version of you is your true authentic self. It's the person who is buried deep down inside of your soul begging to be discovered and set free. They are the only person who fully knows and understands who you currently are, and they are exactly the person who you want to be.

BELOW IS AN EXAMPLE TEMPLATE FOR YOU TO USE OR FEEL FREE TO CREATE YOUR OWN:

Dear [Your Name],
It's me, your future self, and I am writing to you from the future to offer you some words of encouragement and support. I know that life can be tough at times, and it may feel like everything is going wrong. From time to time, you may feel frustrated, anxious, or uncertain about what the future holds. However, I want you to know that everything will work out in the end just as long as you keep pushing forwards. I want you to remember that you are much stronger than you sometimes think, and that you have the ability to overcome any obstacle that may come your way. So, keep pushing through the tough times and know that the best is yet to come!
I know that you have big dreams and aspirations that may seem way out of reach right now, and at times you can feel extremely overwhelmed and discouraged, but I want you to keep believing in yourself no matter what, because you have the skills and the drive to make your dreams a reality. Don't give up on those dreams because they are worth fighting for. Just know that every setback you are faced with is an opportunity to learn and grow for an even bigger

comeback, and that every obstacle you overcome will bring you one step closer to achieving your goals.

Always remember to take care of yourself both physically and mentally because your health is important, and you need to prioritise it. Take time for self-care and remember to always be kind to yourself, especially on the most difficult of days.

Finally, I want you to know that I am proud of you and want you to understand that you are not alone. You are loved and supported the whole way throughout this crazy journey by me and those closest to you. You have come so far and accomplished so much already, so keep pushing forward and never give up on your dreams. I know that you have such a bright future ahead of you, and I can't wait to finally meet you here at the top!

With love and support,

[Your Future Self]

Use everything you have learned throughout this manual to not only create the life of your dreams, but to also inspire and empower others to do the same. Practice all the skills you learned and remember that the road to success is always under construction. This is a never-ending journey of struggle, growth, and success which will require you to take consistent uncomfortable actions in order to see any significant results. Focus on delayed gratification and don't be in such a rush to reach your big goals before you are actually ready. This is because sometimes we learn so much about ourselves along the journey that we end up discovering we want something completely different to what we initially first thought. Understand that fear, worry, and doubt are often signs that you are on the right track, because imposter syndrome is an uncomfortable feeling which is letting you know that you are pushing yourself through the barrier to break into your next level of life. Always remember to be grateful for every single thing that comes your way, both good and bad, but mainly the bad as that is where all of the priceless life lessons are hiding.

Lastly, I want to remind you that when you die, you won't be remembered for the amount of money that was in your bank account, the amount of likes or followers you had on social media, or the fancy things you owned, because all of that S-H-I-T means nothing when you're lying there in a box. You will however be remembered for who you were as a person, how you made others feel, and for all the love you shared with the world throughout your journey. This is because the true secret to fully living is actually giving.

"What do you want people to say about you at your funeral?"

CONGRATULATIONS

Huge congratulations to you for completing this book and all the tasks and challenges that are found within it. I really hope that you've managed to have a completely different view to your life, as well as your future goals, plans, and visions. I also trust that by working through each chapter you've managed to realise and repair any past pain, to replace any potential negative beliefs and habits with more empowering ones, and that you have also gained more clarity for what it is that you want to achieve in your life.

Now you are equipped with the tools that can be used to not only help build the solid foundations for your life, but to also go on and continuously work on yourself to improve your life. Remember that there is no real rush, just as long as you're making micro moves on a daily basis, and over time these small actions will grow to become the big results. Realise that there are going to be many S-H-I-T days, but on the other hand there are also going to be countless great days. When you have the good days just remember that it was well worth pushing through the bad ones, and when you have bad days remember that more good ones are just round the corner, and that's why it's necessary to keep moving forwards despite the current challenges. You don't need to prove anything to anybody, you don't need anybody else's permission, nor do you need anybody else to believe in you but yourself. So put up that post, go to that country by yourself, change your career, and do whatever the fuck you want. This is your life, so live it on your terms and conditions.

I urge you to use this guidebook anytime you're feeling stuck, stressed, or lost in your life. Please don't just get to the end of this and then put it on your shelf collecting dust, because it's always good to go over certain chapters to refresh your mind of specific things that can be beneficial to you in each different chapter of your life.

If you enjoyed this and found it added value to your life, and you know someone that you think would enjoy it too, who would also take great value from it, then please do recommend this book to them. I believe this book would make a great gift for someone, so next time you're thinking what to buy a friend or family member for their birthday or Christmas present, then make sure you bear this in mind. Furthermore, if you want to stand out from the crowd and go above and beyond, then feel free to spread your generosity by doing a random act of kindness by buying a book or two and then giving them out to strangers, or to someone you think may need it in this moment of their life.

I wish you a future of fulfilment that's full of peace, prosperity, love, joy, and abundance, and before you go, just remember this:

Life is beautiful. Life is precious. Life is unpredictable. Life is the greatest gift you'll ever receive. Life can be whatever we want it to be. Life is ours. Life is ending...

Don't get to the
end of your life
with regrets!

Are you ready to sort your

S-H-I-T

out?

Printed in Poland
by Amazon Fulfillment
Poland Sp. z o.o., Wrocław

31908576R00184